The Complete W
L₁.

Thoughts on the True Estimation of Living Forces

Immanuel
Kant

A New Translation with Afterword by
Tim Newcomb

Copyright © 2024 Tim Newcomb

Two things fill my mind with new and ever-increasing admiration and awe, the more frequently and persistently my mind is occupied with them: The starry sky above me and the moral law within me.

I must not look for either of them, nor merely suppose them to be veiled in darkness or exuberance, outside my range of vision; I see them before me and connect them directly with the consciousness of my existence.

The first starts from the place I occupy in the outer world of the senses, and extends the connection in which I stand into the immeasurable greatness of worlds upon worlds and systems of systems, and beyond that into the boundless times of their periodic movement, their beginning and continuation...

The second, on the other hand, increases my value as an intelligence infinitely, through my personality, in which the moral law reveals to me a life independent of animality and even of the whole world of the senses, at least as much as can be deduced from the purposeful determination of my existence by this law, which is not limited to the conditions and limits of this life, but goes into infinity.

...The contemplation of the world began with the most marvelous sight that human senses can only ever present, and our intellect, in its wide scope, can only ever tolerate to pursue, and ended - with the interpretation of the stars.

The Critique of Practical Reason

Contents

First main section The power of bodies in general 16

Thoughts on the True Estimation of the Living Forces and Assessment of the Evidence

Preface

*Nihil magis prästandum est, quam ne pecorum ritu sequamur
antecedentium gregem, pergentes, non qua eundum est, sed qua itur.*
Seneca de vita beata. Cap. I

I

I believe I have reason to form so good an opinion of the judgment
of the world to which I submit these pages, that the liberty I take of
contradicting great men will not be interpreted to me as a crime.
There was a time when one had much to fear from such an
undertaking, but I imagine that time is now past, and that the human
mind has already happily cast off the fetters which ignorance and
admiration once put upon it. Now one can boldly dare to regard the
reputation of Newton and Leibniz as nothing, if it should oppose the
discovery of truth, and to obey no other persuasions than the course
of reason.

II

If I undertake to reject the thoughts of von Leibniz, Wolffen,
Hermann, Bernoulli, Bülfinger, and others, and to give preference to
my own, I should not like to have worse judges than these, for I
know that their judgment, if it rejected my opinions, would not
condemn their intention. No more excellent praise can be given to
these men than that all opinions, without excluding their own, may
be unabashedly censured before them. A moderation of this kind,
though on another occasion, was very creditable to a great man of
antiquity. Timoleon, notwithstanding the services he had rendered
for the freedom of Syracuse, was once called before the court. The
judges were indignant at the presumptuousness of his accusers. But
Timoleon took a very different view of this coincidence. Such an
undertaking could not displease a man who took great pleasure in
seeing his fatherland in the most perfect freedom. He protected those
who used their freedom even against himself. All antiquity has
accompanied this procedure with praise.

After such great efforts made by the greatest men for the freedom of the human mind, should one have reason to fear that they would be displeased with their success?

III

I shall use this moderation and equity to my advantage. But I shall find them only where the marks of merit and excellence of scholarship are prominent. Besides these, there is still a great multitude over whom the prejudice and reputation of great men still exercise a cruel dominion. These gentlemen, who would like to be regarded as arbiters of scholarship, seem to be very skillful in passing judgment on a book without having read it. To expose it to censure, one must only show them its title. If the author is unknown, without character or merit, the book is not worth spoiling the time with; still more if he undertakes great things, to censure famous men, to improve sciences, and to advertise his own thoughts to the world. If it were a question of numbers before the tribunal of science, I should have a very desperate case. But the danger does not make me uneasy. These are they who, as they say, dwell only down on the Parnassus, who have no property and no voice in the election.

IV

Prejudice is rightly made for man; it encourages convenience and self-love, two qualities that cannot be discarded without humanity. He who is taken with prejudices raises certain men, whom it would be in vain to belittle and lower to himself, above all others to an unearthly height. This advantage covers all the rest with the appearance of perfect equality, and makes him unaware of the difference which still prevails among them, and which would otherwise expose him to the vexatious observation of seeing how often one is still surpassed by those who are still within mediocrity. So as long as the vanity of the human mind will still be powerful, so long will prejudice remain, i.e. it will never cease.

V

In the prosecution of this treatise I shall have no hesitation in frankly rejecting the proposition of any man, however famous, if it appears to my mind to be false. This freedom will bring me very hateful consequences. The world is very apt to believe that he who, in one case or another, believes himself to have a more correct knowledge than, say, a great scholar, is in his imagination even superior to him. I venture to say that this appearance is very deceptive, and that it is really deceptive here.

There is no such proportion and similarity in the perfection of the human mind as there is in the structure of the human body. In the latter it is indeed possible to deduce the size of the whole from the size of one member and another; but in the faculty of the intellect it is quite otherwise. Science is an irregular body, without symmetry and uniformity. A scholar of dwarf size often surpasses another in this or that part of knowledge, who nevertheless towers far above him with the whole scope of his science. The vanity of man does not, to all appearance, extend so far that it should not be aware of this difference, and consider the insight of one and another truth to be the same as the broad concept of excellent knowledge; least of all, I know that I would be wronged if I were accused of this.

VI

The world is not so unrighteous as to think that a scholar of rank is no longer subject to the danger of error. But since a low and unknown writer has avoided these errors
from which all his sagacity could not save a great man, that is the difficulty which is not so easily digested. There is much presumption in these words: the truth, for which the greatest masters of human knowledge have vainly striven, first presented itself to my mind. I dare not justify this thought, but I would not willingly deny it.

VII

I am under the impression that it is sometimes not useless to place a certain noble confidence in one's own powers. A confidence of this kind enlivens all our efforts and gives them a certain impetus, which is very conducive to the investigation of the truth. If one is in a condition to persuade oneself that one may still have some confidence in one's observation, and that it is possible to catch a Mr. von Leibniz in error, one does everything in one's power to make one's supposition true. Now, after one has gone astray a thousand times in an undertaking, the gain which has thereby accrued to the knowledge of truths will nevertheless be much more considerable than if one had always kept to the main road.

I base myself on this. I have already mapped out the course I want to follow. I shall set out on my course, and nothing shall hinder me from continuing it.

VIII

There is a new objection that will be made to me, and which, it seems, I must anticipate. I shall sometimes be heard in the tone of a man who is well assured of the correctness of his propositions, and who does not fear that he will be contradicted, or that his conclusions may deceive him. I am not so vain as to imagine this to be the case, nor have I any reason to be so careful in denying to my propositions the appearance of error; for after so many errors to which the human mind has at all times been subjected, it is no longer a disgrace to have erred. There is a quite different intention behind my procedure. The reader of these sheets is doubtless already prepared by the doctrines now in vogue of the living powers before he turns to my treatise. He knows what was thought before Leibniz announced his estimate of forces to the world, and the thought of this man must already be known to him. He has infallibly allowed himself to be won over by the conclusions of one of the two parties, and to all appearances this is the Leibnizian party, for all Germany has now declared its allegiance to it. It is in this frame of mind that he reads these papers. The defense of the living powers has taken over his whole soul under the guise of geometrical proofs. He therefore regards my thoughts only as doubts, and, if I am very fortunate, even as apparent doubts, the resolution of which he leaves to time, and which nevertheless cannot be an obstacle to the truth. On the other hand, I must use all my skill to hold the reader's attention a little longer. I must present myself to him in all the light of conviction which my evidence affords me, in order to draw his attention to the reasons which inspire me with this confidence.

If I were to present my thoughts only under the name of doubt, the world, which is anyway inclined to regard them as nothing better, would very easily be over them; for an opinion which one once believes to have been proved will remain in favor for a very long time, however apparent the doubts by which it is challenged may be and however easily they can be resolved.

A writer generally draws his reader into the state in which he himself was when he wrote his work. I would therefore, if it were possible, rather communicate to him the state of conviction than of doubt; for the latter would be more advantageous to me, and perhaps to the truth, than the former. These are the little tricks which I must not now despise in order to restore the balance of the scales to some extent, in which the reputation of great men has such a powerful influence.

IX

The last difficulty I wish to remove is that which will be made against me for rudeness. It seems that I could have treated the men whom I have undertaken to refute with more deference than I have done. I should have pronounced my judgment of their propositions in a much softer tone. I should not have called them errors, falsehoods, or even delusions. The harshness of these expressions seems belittling to the great names against which they are directed. In the time of distinctions, which was also the time of roughness of manners, one would have replied that the propositions must be judged apart from all the personal merits of their authors. But the politeness of this century imposes a quite different law upon me. I should not be excused if the manner of my expression offended the respect which the merit of great men demands of me. But I am assured that this is not so. If we meet with manifest errors beside the greatest discoveries, it is not a fault of man, but rather of mankind; and one would do too much honor to the person of scholars if one were to exclude them altogether. A great man who erects an edifice of propositions cannot turn his attention equally to all possible sides. He is particularly involved in a certain contemplation, and it is no wonder if errors then escape him from some other side, which he would infallibly have avoided if he had only directed his attention to this outside of this occupation.

I will only confess the truth without equivocation. I shall not be disinclined to consider those propositions as real errors and falsities which appear in my contemplation under this guise; and why should I force myself to conceal this thought so anxiously in my writing, in order to make appear what I do not think, but which the world would like me to think?

And to speak in general, I would also be ill at ease with the ceremony of imparting to all my judgments, which I pronounce on great men, a certain sweep of artfulness, of softening the expressions skillfully, and of showing everywhere the mark of deference; this endeavor would often bring me into a vexatious strait-jacket on account of the choice of words, and subject me to the necessity of digressing beyond the footpath of the philosophical contemplation of all. I shall therefore take the opportunity of this preliminary report to make a public declaration of the reverence and esteem which I shall always entertain for the great masters of our knowledge, whom I shall now have the honor to call my opponents, and which the freedom of my bad judgments cannot in the least detract from.

X

After the various prejudices which I have now endeavored to dispel, there still remains, nevertheless, a certain legitimate prejudice, to which I owe in particular that which might still be found convincing in my writing. If many great men of proven sagacity and power of judgment are led partly by different, partly by the same ways to the assertion of the same proposition, it is a more probable supposition that their proofs are correct, than that the mind of any bad writer should have observed the acuteness in them more accurately. The latter has therefore great reason to make the reproach of his consideration particularly clear and even, to break it down and set it apart in such a way that, if he perhaps commits an error of reasoning, it must immediately shine in his eyes; for it is assumed that, if the consideration is equally intricate, the one who is ahead of the other in perspicacity will sooner discover the truth. He must therefore, as much as possible, make his examination simple and easy, so that, according to the measure of his power of judgment, he may suspect as much light and correctness in his examination as the other, according to the measure of his own, in a much more involved examination.

I have made this observation a law in the execution of my purpose, as will soon be seen.

XI

Before concluding this preliminary report, let us make ourselves acquainted with the present state of the controversy of the living powers.

To all appearances, Mr. von Leibniz did not first see the living forces in the cases in which he first presented them to the world. The beginning of an opinion is generally much simpler, especially of an opinion which involves something so bold and marvelous as that of estimation by the square. We have certain experiences which are very common, and by which we perceive that a real motion, e.g. a blow or push, always carries with it more force than a dead pressure, if it is equally strong. This observation was perhaps the seed of an idea which could not remain unfruitful under the hands of Mr. von Leibniz, and which after his hand grew into the greatness of one of the most famous doctrines.

XII

To speak in general, the matter of the living powers seems, so to speak, to be quite made for the intellect to be seduced by it, even at a time it might have wanted to be. The overpowered obstacles of gravity, the dislocated matter, the compressed springs, the moving masses, the velocities arising in compound motion, all concur in a marvelous way to bring about the appearance of estimation by the square. There is a time when the multiplicity of proofs is that which would make them so sharp and clear. this time is now present among the defenders of the living powers. if they feel little conviction in one or the other of their proofs, the appearance of truth, which, on the other hand, is all the more apparent, strengthens their applause and does not allow it to waver.

XIII

It is more difficult to say on which side the presumption of victory has thus far been most evident in the controversy of the living powers. The two gentlemen Bernoulli, Herr von Leibniz and Hermann, who stood at the head of the philosophers of their nation, could not be outweighed by the reputation of the other scholars of Europe. These men, who had all the weapons of geometry in their power, were alone able to uphold an opinion which might not have been allowed to appear if it had been in the hands of a less famous defender.

Both the party of Cartesius and that of Mr. von Leibniz have felt for their opinion all the conviction of which one is generally only capable in human knowledge. Both parties have sighed at nothing but the prejudice of their opponents, and each party has believed that their opinion could not possibly be doubted if their opponents would only take the trouble to consider it in a proper balance of sentiments.

There is, however, a certain peculiar difference between the way in which the party of the living powers seeks to maintain itself, and the way in which Cartesius' estimate defends itself. The latter appeals only to simple cases, in which the decision of truth and error is easy and certain; the latter, on the contrary, makes its proofs as intricate and obscure as possible, and saves itself, so to speak, by the aid of night, from a combat in which, perhaps, in a proper light of clearness, it would always draw the short straw.

The Leibnizians also have almost all experience on their side; this is perhaps the only thing they have ahead of the Cartesians. Messrs. Poleni, s'Gravesande and van Musschenbroek have rendered them this service, the consequences of which would perhaps be excellent if they had been used more correctly.

In this preliminary report I shall not give an account of what I intend to do in the present treatise on the subject of living forces. This book has no other hope of being read than that which it builds on its brevity; it will therefore be easy for the reader to make himself acquainted with its epitome.

If I might trust to my own imagination, I would say that my opinions might do some not uncomfortable work in settling one of the greatest divisions now existing among the geometrists of Europe. But this persuasion is vain: a man's judgment is nowhere less valid than in his own cause. I am not so much in favor of mine as to give ear to a prejudice of self-love. However, whatever the case may be, I venture to predict with confidence that this dispute will either be settled in a short time or it will never end.

First main section The power of bodies in general

§ 1 Bodies have an essential power

Because I believe that it can contribute something to the intention I have of making the doctrine of living forces certain and decisive, if I have first established some metaphysical concepts of the power of bodies in general, I will begin here.

It is said that a body in motion has a force. For overcoming obstacles, stretching springs, moving masses: all the world calls this working. If one sees no farther than the senses teach, this power is thought to be something which has been communicated to the body entirely from without, and of which it has nothing when it is at rest. The whole body of philosophers before Leibniz was of this opinion, with the exception of Aristotle. It is believed that this man's dark entelechy is the secret of the effects of bodies. The school teachers as a whole, who all followed Aristotle, did not understand this enigma, and perhaps it was not made to be understood by anyone. Leibniz, to whom human reason owes so much, first taught that the body possesses an essential power, which comes to it even before extension. Est aliquid präter extensionem imo extensione prius; these are his words.

§ 2 Leibniz called this force of bodies the acting force in general. The inventor called this force by the general name of the acting force. One should only have followed him in the doctrinal buildings of metaphysics; but one has sought to define this force somewhat more precisely. The body, it is said, has a moving force, for it is seen to do nothing else but produce motion. When it pushes, it strives to move; only then is the force in exercise, when the movement is real. I maintain, however, that if we attribute to the body an essential moving force (vim motricem) in order to have an answer to the question of the cause of motion ready, we are to a certain extent practicing the artifice which the school teachers made use of by resorting to a vi calorifica or frigifaciente in the investigation of the causes of heat or cold.

§ 3 It is fair to call the soft power vin activam

One does not speak correctly if one makes movement a kind of effect and therefore attaches to it a force of the same name. A body to which infinitely little resistance occurs, which therefore acts almost not at all, has the most motion. Motion is only the external phenomenon of the state of the body, since it does not act, but endeavors to act; only when it suddenly loses its motion through an object, that is the moment it is brought to rest, then it acts. Hence the force of a substance should not be called that which is not an effect at all, much less should it be said of bodies which act when at rest (e.g. of a ball which presses the table on which it lies by its weight) that they make an effort to move. For since they would then not act if they moved, one would have to say that, by acting, a body has an effort to get into the state in which it does not act. The force of a body should therefore be called a vim activam rather than a vim motricem.

§ 4 How the movement can be explained from the active force in general.

But nothing is easier than to deduce the origin of what we call motion from the general concepts of active force. Substance A, whose power is determined to act outside itself (that is, to change the inner state of other substances), either immediately finds, at the first moment of its endeavor, an object that endures its whole power, or it does not find such an object. If the former were true of all substances, we would know no motion at all, and we would therefore not be able to name the power of the bodies of it. But if substance A cannot exert all its power at the moment of its effort, it will exert only a part of it. But it cannot remain inactive with the remaining part of it. On the contrary, it must act with its whole force, for otherwise it would cease to be called a force if it were not fully applied. Therefore, because the consequences of this exercise are not to be found in the coexistent state of the world, they will have to be found in the second dimension of it, namely in the successive series of things. The body will therefore not apply its power all at once, but gradually. However, in the following moments it cannot act in the same substances in which it acted at first, for these only endure the first part of its force, but are incapable of accepting the rest; thus A always acts gradually in other substances. But substance C, into which it acts at the second moment, must have a quite different relation of place and position to A than B, into which it acted at the very beginning, for otherwise there would be no reason why A should not have acted at once at the beginning both into substance C and into B. In the same way, the substances into which it acts in subsequent moments each have a different position in relation to the first location of body A. That is, A changes its location by acting successively.

§ 5 What difficulties flow from this into the doctrine of the action of the body in the soul, if no other force vim motricem is attached to it

Because we are not clearly aware of what a what kind of body does when it acts in a state of rest, we always think back to the movement that would take place if the resistance were removed. It would be enough to make use of it in order to have an external character of that which takes place in the body and which we cannot see. But the movement is generally regarded as that which the force does when it breaks loose, and which is the only result of it. Because it is so easy to find one's way back from this slight deviation to the right concept, one should not think that such an error would be of consequence. But it is indeed, although not in mechanics and natural theories. For this is precisely why it is so difficult in metaphysics to imagine how matter is capable of producing ideas in the soul of man in a way that is actually effective (that is, through physical influence). What else does matter do, it is said, but cause motion? Therefore all its power will amount to the fact that at most it moves the soul out of its place. But how is it possible that the force which alone produces motion should produce conceptions and ideas? These are such different kinds of things that it is incomprehensible how one could be the source of the other.

§ 6 The difficulty arises when we speak of the action of the soul in the body. And this can be raised by calling it vis activa.

The same difficulty arises when the question is whether the soul is also capable of setting matter in motion. Both difficulties disappear from this, however, and the physical influence receives no little light, if the power of matter is not placed on that of the effect account of motion, but of the effects in other substances, which cannot be more closely defined. For the question whether the soul can cause movements, that is, whether it has a moving power, is transformed into this: whether its essential power can be determined to have an effect outwards, that is, whether it is capable of acting outside itself in other beings and bringing about changes? This question can be answered in a very decisive way by saying that the soul must be able to act outwards for this reason, because it is in a place. For if we dissect the concept of what we call place, we find that it indicates the effects of the substances in each other. Nothing, then, has more prevented a certain astute writer from perfecting the triumph of physical influence over predestined harmony than this little confusion of concepts, from which it is easy to find one's way out as soon as one turns one's attention to it.

If we call the power of bodies a real power, it is easy to understand how matter could determine the soul to certain ideas.

It is just as easy to understand the nature of the paradoxical proposition, namely, how it is possible that matter, of which it is imagined that it can cause nothing but motion, can impress certain ideas and images on the soul. For matter, which has been set in motion, affects everything that is connected with it in space, and therefore also the soul; that is, it changes the inner state of the soul in so far as it relates to the outer. Now the whole inward state of the soul is nothing else than the summary of all its ideas and concepts, and in so far as this inward state relates to the external, it is called the status representativus universi ; therefore matter, by means of the power it has in motion, changes the state of the soul by which it imagines the world. In this way one understands how it can impress ideas on the soul.

§ 7 Things can really exist and yet not be present anywhere in the world

It is difficult not to digress in a matter of such vast extent; but I must only return to what I wanted to say about the power of bodies. Since all connection and relation of substances existing apart from each other derives from the reciprocal effects which their forces exert upon each other, let us see what truths can be deduced from this concept of force. Either a substance is in a connection and relation with others besides itself, or it is not. Since every independent being contains within itself the complete source of all its determinations, it is not necessary for its existence that it should be in connection with other things. Therefore substances can exist and yet have no external relation to others, or be in any real connection with them. Since there is no place without external connections, positions and relations, it is certainly possible for a thing to really exist and yet not be present anywhere in the whole world. This paradoxical proposition, although it is a consequence, and indeed a very easy consequence, of the best known truths, has, as far as I know, never yet been remarked upon by any one. But there are other propositions flowing from the same source which are no less marvelous and, so to speak, take hold of the mind against its will.

§ 8 It is true in the right metaphysical sense that more than one world can exist.

Since something cannot be said to be a part of a whole if it has no connection at all with the other parts (for otherwise there would be no difference between a real union and an imaginary one), but the world is a really composite being, a substance that is not connected with any thing in the whole world will not belong to the world at all, except in thought, that is, it will not be a part of it. If there are many such beings, which are not connected with any thing in the world, but only have a relation to one another, then a very special whole arises from this, they make up a very special world. It is therefore not correct to say in the lecture halls of worldly wisdom that in the metaphysical sense there can no longer be such a thing as a single world. It is really possible that God has created many millions of worlds, even taken in a quite metaphysical sense; therefore it remains undecided whether they really exist or not. The error which has been committed in this respect has infallibly arisen because no exact attention has been paid to the explanation of the world. For the definition reckons to the world only that which has a real connection with the other things, but the theorem forgets this restriction and speaks of all existing things in general.

§ 9 It is true in the right metaphysical sense that more than one world can exist.

Since one cannot say that something is a part of a whole if it has no connection at all with the other parts (for otherwise there would be no difference between a real union and an imaginary one), but the world is a really composed being, then a substance that is not connected with any thing in the whole world will not belong to the world at all, except in thought, that is, it will not be a part of it. If there are many such beings, which are not connected with any thing in the world, but only have a relation to one another, then a very special whole arises from this, they make up a very special world. It is therefore not correct to say in the lecture halls of worldly wisdom that in the metaphysical sense there can no longer be such a thing as a single world. It is really possible that God has created many millions of worlds, even taken in a quite metaphysical sense; therefore it remains undecided whether they really exist or not. The error which has been committed in this respect has infallibly arisen because no exact attention has been paid to the explanation of the world. For the definition reckons to the world only that which has a real connection with the other things, but the theorem forgets this limitation and speaks of all existing things in general.

§ 10 It is probable that the threefold dimension of space derives from the law according to which the forces of substances act upon one another.

Since everything that occurs among the properties of a thing must be derivable from that which contains within itself the complete ground of the thing itself, so also the properties of extension, and therefore also the threefold measurement of it, will be based on the properties of the force which the substances possess with respect to the things with which they are connected. The force with which a substance acts in union with others cannot be conceived without a certain law, which manifests itself in the nature of its action. Since the nature of the law by which the substances act in each other must also determine the nature of the union and composition of many of them, the law by which a whole collection of substances (that is, a space) is measured, or the dimension of extension, will derive from the laws by which the substances seek to unite by virtue of their essential powers.

The threefold dimension seems to stem from the fact that the substances in the existing world act upon one another in such a way that the strength of the effect is inversely proportional to the square of the distance.

According to this I hold that that the substances in the existing world, of which we are a part, have essential powers of such a kind that, in union with each other, they spread out their effects from themselves according to the double inverse ratio of the widths; secondly, that the whole, which therefore springs from this law, has the property of the threefold dimension; thirdly, that this law is arbitrary, and that God could have chosen another for it, as an example of the inverse threefold relation; finally, fourthly, that from another law an extension of other properties and dimensions would also have flowed. A science of all these possible kinds of space would infallibly be the highest geometry that a finite mind could undertake.

The impossibility we notice in ourselves of imagining a space of more than three dimensions seems to me to arise from the fact that our soul also receives impressions from outside according to the law of the inverse double ratio of distances, and because its nature itself is made not only to suffer in this way, but also to act outside itself in this way.

§ 11 Some teachers of metaphysics maintain that the body exists by virtue of its power to move in all directions.

The latest worldly wisdom establishes certain concepts of the essential power of bodies which cannot, however, be accepted. It is called a perpetual tendency to motion. Besides the error # of the body which this notion, as I have shown at the outset, carries with it, there is another which I shall now speak of # force. If force is a perpetual effort # to act in all areas, it would be an obvious contradiction # to motion if one were to say that this effort of force is completely undetermined with respect to external things. For by virtue of its definition it endeavors to work outside itself into other things; indeed, according to the supposed doctrines of the latest teachers of metaphysics, it really does work into them. Hence those seem to speak most correctly who say that it is rather directed towards all regions than that it is altogether indeterminate as to direction. The famous Mr. Hamberger therefore maintains that the substantial force of the monads strives to move in the same way in all directions, and therefore, like a balance, maintains itself at rest through the equality of the counter-pressures.

§ 12 Some teachers of metaphysics maintain that the body exists by virtue of its power to move in all directions.

The latest worldly wisdom establishes certain concepts of the essential power of bodies which cannot, however, be accepted. It is called a perpetual tendency to motion. Besides the error # of the body which this notion, as I have shown at the outset, carries with it, there is another which I shall now speak of # force. If force is a perpetual effort # to act in all areas, it would be an obvious contradiction # to motion if one were to say that this effort of force is completely undetermined with respect to external things. For by virtue of its definition it endeavors to work outside itself into other things; indeed, according to the supposed doctrines of the latest teachers of metaphysics, it really does work into them. Hence those seem to speak most correctly who say that it is rather directed towards all regions than that it is altogether indeterminate as to direction. The famous Mr. Hamberger, therefore, maintains that the substantial force of the monads strives to move in the same way in all directions and therefore, like a balance, maintains itself in rest through the equality of the counter-pressures.

§ 13 First objection to this opinion.

According to this system, motion arises when the equilibrium of two opposite tendencies is established, and the body moves in the direction of the greater tendency with the excess of force which it has received over the smaller opposite tendency. This explanation satisfies the imagination even in the case where the moving body always moves away at the same time as the moving body. For this case is similar to that in which someone supports one of two equally weighted scales with his hand and thereby causes the movement of the other. But a body whose motion has been imparted to it by a push will continue to do so indefinitely, even though the driving force ceases to act in it. According to the above doctrine, however, it would not be able to continue its motion, but as soon as the driving body ceased to act in it, it would suddenly come to rest. For since the tendencies of the force of the body, directed in all directions, are inseparable from its substance, the equilibrium of these tendencies will be restored the moment the external force, which had opposed one tendency, ceases to act.

§ 14 Second objection to the same opinion.

But this is not the only difficulty. Because a thing must be determined throughout, the tendency to movement which the substances exert in all directions must have a certain degree of intensity. For it cannot be infinite; but a finite effort to work without a certain magnitude of effort is impossible. Therefore, because the degree of intensity is finite and definite, suppose that a body A of equal mass were to run against it with a force three times greater than all the effort to move it has in the essential force of its substance: it will only be able to take away the third part of its velocity from the running body through its vim inertiae; but it will not itself attain a greater velocity than that which is equal to the third part of the velocity of the moving body. After the impact has been made, therefore, A, as the approaching body, will move with two degrees of velocity, but B will only move with one degree in the same direction. Now because B stands in the way of body A and does not assume as much velocity as it needs in order not to hinder the motion of body A; because, despite this, it is not able to stop the latter's motion: so A will really move in the direction AC with velocity 2, but B, which is in the way of body A, will move in this same direction with a velocity like 1, but movements on both sides will nevertheless proceed unhindered. This is impossible, however, unless one wanted to posit that B is penetrated by A, which is a metaphysical inconsistency.

§ 15 Body has an essential force Double division of motion.

It is time for me to finish this metaphysical preparation. I cannot, however, refrain from adding a remark which I consider indispensable for the understanding of what follows. The notions of the dead pressure and of the measure of it, which occur in mechanics, I presuppose in my readers, and in general I shall not present in these sheets a complete treatise of all that belongs to the doctrine of living and dead forces; but only sketch a few minor thoughts which seem to me to be new and conducive to my main intention of improving Leibniz's measure of forces. I therefore divide all movements into two main types. The one has the property that it maintains itself in the body to which it has been imparted and continues indefinitely if no obstacle opposes it. The other is a perpetual effect of a constantly impulsive force, which does not even require resistance to destroy it, but is based only on the external force and disappears as soon as the latter ceases to sustain it. An example of the first kind is the shot ball and all thrown bodies; of the second kind is the motion of a ball gently pushed by the hand, or otherwise all bodies that are carried or pulled with moderate speed.

§ 16 The movement of the first kind is indistinguishable from dead pressure.

It is easy to understand, without entering into a deep consideration of metaphysics, that the force which expresses itself in the motion of the first kind has something infinite in comparison with the force of the second kind. For the latter partly annihilates itself and suddenly ceases of its own accord as soon as the motive power withdraws; it can therefore be regarded as if it disappeared every moment, but is just as often produced again, whereas the former is an inner source of an inherently imperishable force that performs its effect in a perpetual time. It thus relates to the former as a moment relates to time, or as a point relates to a line. A motion of this kind is therefore indistinguishable from the dead pressure, as Baron Wolff has already remarked in his Cosmology.

§ 17 Motion of the second kind presupposes a force that behaves like the square of velocity.

Since I want to speak of motion as actually maintaining itself in an empty space in eternity, I shall consider the nature of it in a few words according to the concepts of metaphysics. If a body runs in free motion in an infinitely subtle space, its force can be measured according to the sum of all the effects it performs in eternity. For if this aggregate were not equal to its whole force, then, in order to find a sum equal to the whole intensity of the force, one would have to take a longer time than infinite time, which is inconsistent. If we now compare two bodies A and B, of which A has a velocity of 2, but B a velocity of 1, then A, from the beginning of its motion, pushes the infinitely small masses of the space through which it passes with twice as much velocity as B. But in this infinite time it also pushes the infinitely small masses of the space through which it passes with twice as much velocity, but in this infinite time it also covers a space twice as large as B, so the whole magnitude of the effect which A performs is proportional to the product of the force with which it encounters the small parts of space in the quantity of these parts, and the same is true of the force of B. Now both their actions in the small molecules of space are proportioned to their velocities, and the quantity of these parts are likewise like the velocities, consequently the magnitude of the whole action of one body to the whole action of the other is like the square of their velocities, and therefore their forces are also in this proportion.

§ 18 Second reason hereof.

For a better conception of this property of the living forces, one can think back to what was said in the 16th §. The dead pressures can have nothing more than simple velocity as their measure; for since their force does not rest on the bodies which exert it, but is exerted by an external force, the resistance which overpowers it has no need of a certain special effort in regard to the strength with which this force seeks to maintain itself in the body (for the force is in no way rooted in the acting substance and endeavors to maintain itself in it), but it has need only of destroying the single velocity which the body uses to change its place. But it is quite different with the living force. Because the state in which the substance finds itself, in that it proceeds in free motion at a certain speed, is entirely based on the internal determinations, the same substance at the same time endeavors to maintain itself in this state. The external resistance, therefore, must at the same time, besides the force which it requires to counterbalance the velocity of this body, have a special power to break the effort with which the internal force of the body is exerted to maintain in itself this state of motion, and the whole strength of the resistance, which is to bring bodies in free motion to rest, must therefore be in compound proportion from the proportion of the velocity and the force with which the body endeavors to maintain this state of effort in itself; i. e. because both ratios are equal to each other. i. because both ratios are equal, the force required for resistance is the square of the velocity of the moving body.

§ 19

I must not promise myself to obtain anything decisive and incontrovertible in a consideration which is merely metaphysical, therefore I turn to the following chapter, which, by the application of mathematics, will perhaps be able to make more claims to conviction. Our metaphysics, like many other sciences, is indeed only on the threshold of a fairly thorough knowledge; God knows when it will be seen to pass it. It is not difficult to see its weakness in some of the things it undertakes. Prejudice is very often found to be the greatest strength of her evidence. Nothing is more to blame for this than the prevailing tendency of those who seek to extend human knowledge. They would like to have a great wisdom of the world, but it would be desirable that it should be a thorough one. It is almost the only recompense a philosopher can get for his efforts when, after a laborious investigation, he can finally rest easy in the possession of a fairly thorough science. It is therefore very much to be expected of him that he should seldom trust his own applause, that he should not conceal in his own discoveries the imperfections which he is unable to improve, and that he should never be so vain as to set aside the true utility of knowledge for the pleasure which the imagination derives from a thorough science. The intellect is very prone to envy, and it is, of course, very difficult to hold it back for a long time; but one should at last be compelled to do so in order to sacrifice everything that has a far-reaching appeal to a well-founded knowledge.

Second main section Examination of the doctrines of the Leibnizian party on the living forces.

§ 20

In the treatise which Mr. Bülfinger presented to the Petersburg Academy, I find a consideration which I have always used as a rule in the investigation of truths. When men of good sense, in whom either on neither or on both sides the presumption of alien intentions is to be found, assert opinions quite contrary to each other, it is according to the logic of probabilities to direct one's attention most to a certain middle proposition which leaves both parties to some extent right.

§ 21.

I do not know whether I have otherwise been happy in this way of thinking, but in the controversy about the living forces I hope to be so. Never has the world been more divided in certain opinions than in those concerning the measure of the forces of moving bodies. The parties are, in all respects, equally strong and equally fair. Foreign intentions may, of course, interfere, but of which party can it be said that it is entirely free from them? I therefore choose the safest course by taking an opinion in which both great parties find their account.

§ 22 Leibnizen's and Descarte's estimate of the powers.

Before Leibnizen, the world had paid homage to the single theorem of Descarte, which gave to bodies, even those in actual motion, only mere velocities as the measure of their force. No one thought it possible to place any doubt in this; but Leibniz, by the promulgation of a new law, suddenly threw human reason into indignation, which in after times has become one of those which have presented the greatest contest of wits to the learned. Descarte had estimated the forces of moving bodies according to their velocities per se, but Mr. Leibniz took the square of their velocity as their measure. This rule of his he did not, as one might think, propound only under certain conditions which still allowed some room for the previous one; no, but he denied Descart's law absolutely and without qualification, and immediately substituted his own for it.

§ 23 First error of Leibniz's measure of forces.

There are actually two things that I find fault with von Leibniz's rule. That of which I shall now speak has no consequences of importance in the matter of living forces; but it cannot, nevertheless, be omitted to be remarked, lest in so great a proposition nothing should be omitted which can exonerate it from all small reproaches which might be brought against it.

§ 24 What a real movement is.

I shall now make the second remark, which will reveal to us the sources of the infamous controversy, and which perhaps also offers the only means of settling it.

The defenders of the new estimate of living forces are still in agreement with the Cartesians in this, that bodies, when their motion is only in the beginning, possess a force which behaves like their mere velocity. But as soon as motion can be called real, the body, in their opinion, has the square of its velocity as its measure.

Let us now examine what a real motion actually is. For this word was the cause of Cartesian apostasy, but perhaps it can also be a cause of reunion.

A movement is called real when it is not merely in the point of beginning, but when, while it lasts, a time has elapsed. This elapsed time between the beginning of the motion and the moment in which the body acts is what actually makes it possible to call the motion real.

Note, however, that this time is not of set and measured magnitude, but that it is entirely undetermined and can be determined at will. That is, it can be assumed to be as small as one wishes if it is to be used to indicate a real movement. For it is not the magnitude of time that actually makes the movement real, no, it is time in general, be it as small or as great as it will.

§ 25 Second main error of Leibniz's measure of forces.

According to this, the time spent in motion is the true and only character of the living force; and it is this alone which gives it a special measure over the dead one.

Let us now represent the time that elapses from the beginning of motion until the body encounters an object into which it acts, by the line AB, the beginning of which is in A.[1] In B, then, the body has a living force, but it does not have it at the initial point A, for there it would merely push a resistance that stood against it with an effort to move. But let us further conclude as follows. For the

First, the time AB is such a determination of the body which is in B, whereby a living force is placed in it, and the initial point A (namely, when I place the body in it) is a determination which is a ground of the dead force.

If in thought I make this determination, which is expressed by the line AB, smaller, I place the body nearer to the initial point, and it is easy to understand that, if I continued this, the body would finally be in A itself; consequently the determination AB will be placed nearer and nearer to the determination in A by its abbreviation; for if it did not approach it at all, the body could never gain the point A by the abbreviation of time, if I continued it indefinitely, which is incongruous. Thus the determination of the body in C comes nearer to the conditions of the dead force than in B, in D still nearer than in C, and so on, until in A itself it has all the conditions of the dead force, and the conditions of the living force have entirely disappeared.

But if certain determinations, which are the cause of one property of a body, are gradually transformed into other determinations, which are the cause of an opposite property, then the property which was a consequence of the former condition must at the same time change with it and gradually transform itself into that property which is a consequence of the latter. Now since, if I abbreviate the time AB (which is a condition of a living force in B) in thought, this condition of the living force is necessarily placed nearer to the condition of the dead force than it was in B: so also the body in C must really have a force nearer to the dead one than that in B, and nearer still if I place it in D. Accordingly, a body that possesses a living force under the condition of elapsed time does not have it in any time, which can be as short as one wishes; no, it must be determinate and certain, for if it were shorter, it would no longer have this living force. Thus Leibnizen's law of the estimation of forces cannot take place; for it attributes a living force to bodies which have moved for any time at all (this is to say as much as they really move), without distinction, this time may be as short or as long as one pleases.

Afterword by the Translator

The Starry Sky above me and the Moral Law within me: The Recluse Metaphysician of Königsberg

Kant's entire body of work can be understood as a resurrection of the debates between Hellenistic Skepticism and Platonism, the Stoics and the Epicureans, particularly in his attempt to address the limits of human knowledge and understanding. His critical philosophy questioning the ability to know things-in-themselves, aligns with skeptical concerns about the certainty of knowledge gained through the methodology, in light of Cartesian methodology. Kant's ideas about innate knowledge and the existence of non-empirical concepts are an innovation on the Platonic theory of Forms, particularly the concept of noumena (things-in-themselves), is reminiscent of Plato's metaphysics where truest reality, or that which is most meaningful, is not sensory or empirical, but Noetic- Mind-Spirit. This is a return to the Judeo-Platonic continuum where "the fear of the lord is the beginning of all knowledge" (i.e. the material world is unknowable potentiality without the Representative world), and a repudiation of the influence of Aristotle in the middle ages which laid the foundation of Materialistic Protestantism & Atheism. Still, Kant built bridges between his neo-platonic apologetics (aimed against the English Empiricists) and Aristotelian logic, despite his critiques. His categorical imperative has parallels with Aristotle's focus on virtue ethics and the importance of rationality in determining ethical behavior, and a resurrection of Stoicism's unyielding demand of absolute ethical behavior- "even in a palace one can be moral".

The Categorical Imperative might have been new to Epicurean Protestants, but it is merely a new intellectualization of Stoic philosophy. Individual duty towards a transcendent moral law is rather a long-form description of Saintliness, of Holiness. Eastern Orthodoxy's adoption of the Stoic conceptualization of dispassion against the Epicureanism in the 1st century, lost in the great Schism and the subsequent Reformation which further dogmatized morality tethered to nothing but subjective individualistic interpretation of the Bible, was brought back from extinction in Luther and Hume's Empiricism and later Utilitarianism. This is a very old windmill that Kant spent his life tilting at. All of Kant's arguments for absolute morality ring hollow in the Ancient Eastern Churches, which have been practicing this Stoic call towards absolute, Ontologic goodness, manifest in Monasticism. The antinomies that are attributed to Kant are ancient; they are the same antinomies that were lost in the post-

Latin west, but still strongly resound in the Ancient East to this day. Kant's 1763 "*Attempt to Introduce the Concept of Negative Quantities into World Wisdom*" sounds awfully similar to the mystical Apophatic philosophy of the early church, forgotten in the European deviations. The Kingdom of Ends is the Orthodox earthly telos of Byzantium. Imagine if Kant could have walked with the Monks of the Holy Mountain, the only relic of Byzantium in Europe, who were in warfare against this "radical evil" Kant monologued so much about. While central Europe was is the midst of the violence of the religious wars and then the violence of the enlightenment from the French Revolution, Athos was practicing daily the Categorical Imperative.

But where a Protestant returns to orthodox theology in one area, they inevitably deviate in others- Kant, for example, believed that Christians should never pray, as this was a pagan, mystical belief. No Protestant has ever been able to "herd the cats", and the never-ending debates over moral issues between the tens of thousands of Protestant denominations rage just the same today as they did in Kant's day. Even towards the greatest Protestant intellectuals, the Ancient East can only shake its head in pity and frustration. No amount of intellect can result in a morally coherent ideology, no amount of logic can save, and yet, there is the unspoken ethos that mere intellect can alone arrive one at the truth (the Neo-Gnosticism of Luther's *Claritas Scriptura*), despite 500 years of evidence to the contrary. In the East, morality is not merely rationalism, but trust in a Person and a living relationship to that Person; the dogmas of the faith are the beginning, not the end. Yet in the West, morality is merely the result of argumentation and rationalism severed entirely from a personal, kinetic encounter with Goodness Manifest in the Eucharist. Apart from the Eucharistic life, from the dispassion resulting from the Divinization of Theosis, there is no hope of morality, the East repeats to deaf ears across a millennia. This is the lesson of the Great Continental Philosophers. This is their poverty.

The Fate of the Human Condition in the 'Zodiacal Light' of the Cosmogony of the Newtonian Enlightenment

Kant's 1755 *Universal Natural History and Theory of Heaven* is his first major entry into the philosophic world and we see here his initial sketches of his response to Materialistic Determinism which was being developed in an interpretation of Newtonian mechanics. Kant was a central intellect in the Enlightenment but was also heavily critical of the "scientific" developments done apart from Metaphysical thinking. He is concerned that the materialism of the Enlightenment will destroy humanity, rendering Good and Evil merely an opinion, leading to untold horrors. This work is vast and shallow in scope, but by the end of the century, Kant will have sharpened his thinking and criticisms on all of these topics in their own hegemonic philosophic works. By the 1780's he had published his three major critiques of Mechanical Reductionism and laid the groundwork for a universal morality in his final works including the monumental 1797 Metaphysics of Morals.

On strictly a scientific level, Kant's theories of planet formation are strikingly accurate when compared to the theories of his peers. Here he postulates the Nebular Hypothesis on the formation and evolution of planetary systems, which is today the broadly accepted theory of planet formation. Some of his other ideas are naturally a bit nutty (such as the Earth once had rings around it) but his general ideas are surprisingly accurate for his days. He was also correct in his assumption, which was unsubstantiated by observation at the time, that our Milky Way galaxy was only one of countless, which was only confirmed by the Hubble Telescope in the 1920s. He refers to Galaxies as "Welteninsel" or "world islands". He began this exploration into cosmogony after reading Thomas Wright's 1750 "An original theory or new hypothesis of the Universe". This is the epicenter of the chaos of the Enlightenment, and Kant's theories are surprisingly rational and accurate.

Xenoanthropology and Xenobiology were already being widely discussed. He quotes Alexander Pope's "From the inhabitants of the stars" and other academics who discuss the possibility of other Xenoplants, which the Keplar mission has only recently confirmed. Alexander Pope was an English poet, writer, and satirist of the late 17th century. He was a major Enlightenment thinker and one of the most prominent poets of the 18th century, as we can see from Kant's extensive quotations of him. He was a contemporary of Sir Isaac Newton and wrote an epigram for his grave, so it makes sense Kant would rely on his words so heavily when criticizing the misuse of Newtonian physics. Kant's epitaph for the father of Physics reads:

Nature and nature's laws lay hid in night;
God said "Let Newton be!" and all was light.
Nature and nature's laws lay in the dark night;
God said: Newton be! And they shone with splendor.

Kant's work on Natural Philosophy and Anthropology is directly correlated to his core ethical and moral philosophy, for which he is best known. Natural Determinism led to the moral philosophy of Kant's great opponent David Hume, so to attack Humean moral relativism, one must challenge its foundation in the deterministic interpretation of Newtonian physics. Already in this early work focused on Cosmogony, he criticizes the Epistemology of the Enlightenment (which he identifies in the preface as Epicureanism) and the paralogisms of his contemporaries including the Physical Monadology of Leibnitz.

Heidegger warns of trying to describe Kant and Hegel purely in terms of re-interpretations of their predecessors, applying a metaphysical understanding to history, an approach Heidegger wrote tomes on. In his 1923 *"Hegel's Phenomenology"* he writes:

It is therefore by no means sufficient for the understanding that we say: Hegel got the categorial determination of the essence of the thing as force in a certain way from Kant. This statement is correct; but as long as it remains only so correct, it remains meaningless. One can fill volumes with statements about what Aristotle has from Plato, Descartes from Scholasticism, Kant from Leibniz, Hegel from Fichte. But this alleged and supposed exactness of historical determinations is not only superficial; if it were only that, then one could calmly leave it to its unsurpassable complacency and harmlessness. But this historical explanation is also misleading. It pretends to say how it really has been in philosophy, while it is not touched with a breath by the reality of philosophizing. Our statement - the Hegelian determination of the essence of the thing as force goes back to Kant - is correct and meaningless. Nor does it say anything more if we were still to try, for instance, to explain backward the significance of the concept of force for the substantiality of substance from Leibniz and to trace forward the influence of Schelling's philosophy of nature and of the system of transcendental idealism (1800) on Hegel. It depends on how Hegel took all this up, penetrated it and transformed it into his problematics - his not as a personal intellectual product, but his as the factual completion and development of the earlier.

Space-Time as an Archetype

Kant displayed an advanced understanding of the natural sciences including an advanced understanding of what would become Quantum Theory including Space-Time, pushing back against the Leibniz-Wolff conceptualization (a real abstraction of the succession of internal states) and the dominant Newtonian definition (continuous flow in existence without any real basis- a sequence of events).

Newton's ideas were already superseding the previously dominant Leibnizian concepts, and he uncharacteristically insults the idea of time being success as "a most absurd notion". Time is only absolute to Phenomenology, but nothing else. Standing on the other side of the experiments which proved the relativity of time, Kant's arguments here aged well:

Succession does not create the concept of time but rather necessitates it. Therefore, the notion of time, often acquired through experience, is poorly defined as "the series of actual entities succeeding one another." This definition is unclear because understanding 'after' requires a pre-existing concept of time. There are different times for things that exist after each other, just as there are simultaneous times for things that exist at the same time.

The idea of time is singular, not general. Every instance of time is thought of as part of one immense time. When thinking of two years, they cannot be conceptualized except in relation to each other, and if they do not immediately follow one another, there must be a certain time in between. The distinction between seasons as earlier or later cannot be defined based on some characteristic of understanding without falling into circular reasoning. The mind discerns this only through a unique perception. Moreover, every actuality is placed in time, not under a general concept as a common characteristic, but as distinct content.

Thus, the idea of time is a perception, and since it is conceived as a condition of relations in the senses before all sensation, it is not a sensual but a pure view.

Time is a continuous and lawful quantity, continuous in the changes from the beginning of the universe. It is an amount that is not reducible to the simple. Through time, only relations are thought of, without any given beings related to each other. Time, as a composition, when the whole is removed, leaves absolutely nothing. When a composition is removed from all composition, nothing at all remains; it is not reducible to simple parts. Therefore, any part of time is still time, and the entities in time are simple, that is, moments, not parts of time, but limits within which time occurs. For any given two moments in time, they succeed each other to the extent that they actually exist. Thus, a given moment in time necessitates another moment in its succession.

The law of continuity in metaphysics states that all changes are continuous, i.e., they flow, but they do not leap from one state to its opposite without a series of intermediate states. For two states that are opposed in time, there are different moments, but between any two moments, there is always some time, within which an infinite series of moments exists. In this time, a substance is not entirely in one state, nor in the other, nor in none; it exists in various states, and so on ad infinitum.

Heidegger similarly makes a metaphysical case for the truest definition of Space-time:

Space is neither in the subject, nor is the world in space. Rather, space is "in" the world, insofar as being-in-the-world, which is constitutive for existence, has opened up space. Space is not in the subject, nor does the subject view the world "as if" it were in a space, but the ontologically well-understood "subject", the being-in, is spatial. And because existence is spatial in the way described, space appears as a priori. This title does not mean something like a prior affiliation to an initially still worldless subject that throws a space out of itself. Apriority here means: The spatiality of the prudently initially encountered can become thematic for prudence itself and the task of calculation and measurement, for example in house building and land surveying.

The origin of Kant's space-time theory in his initial 1770 dissertation was not merely an abstract philosophical exploration, but was grounded in addressing the practical challenges of conceptualizing absolute space in relation to sensory perception. This is Germaine to his entire project of dialectally reconciling Rationalism and Empiricism. This nuanced understanding of space and time as forms of human sensibility, distinct from their conceptualization in absolute terms, formed a fundamental aspect of Kant's later philosophical endeavors. He writes (originally in Latin):

But the first philosophy, which contains the principles of the pure use of understanding, is metaphysical... Since, therefore, empirical principles are not to be found in Metaphysics, the concept of obstacles should not be sought in the senses, but in the very nature of the not-pure understanding. This understanding is not from the conception of the tried, but from the innate laws of the mind (observing its actions on the occasion of experience), and hence, it is acquired. Of this kind are concepts like possibility, existence, necessity, substance, cause, etc., along with their opposites or correlatives. These concepts never enter as parts of any sensual representation and therefore cannot in any way be abstracted from it.

The *A Priori* forms of sensual experience (Sense-perception) are not directly determined by sensation, but rather we always have one general sensation belonging to sensibility in Space-Time. This distinction is at the heart of Kantian Transcendental Aesthetics.

Beauty as Teleological Rationality Manifest as Purpose

Immanuel Kant's 1764 Observations on the Sense of the Beautiful and the Sublime is his entry into the philosophic field of Aesthetics and provides the framework of his theories on beauty which would be fully enumerated in his 1790 Critique of Judgement. Kant distinguishes between the beautiful and the Subline, which are further divided into Attached (mathematic) and Free (dynamic) Beauty. The beautiful is playful and limited to certain forms, while the sublime is serious and limitless. Beauty inhabits life; the sublime is beyond life. This is a more nuanced, developed form of Edmund Burke's popular theories on Aesthetics.

Aesthetics concerns the knowledge of the beautiful beyond subjective experience. To Kant, sublimity does not exist apart from consciousness. Because of this observation of the Subject, Kant uses the latest personality science to explain how sublimity is manifested in society. In Kant's day, this was the "four temperament theory" which stated that there are four base personality types: sanguine, choleric, melancholic, and phlegmatic. Kant analyses beauty through these constructs, and then makes the same analysis through ethnonational identities- the English, the French, the Germans, the Arabs, the Spaniards, the Persians, the Japanese, Africans, Indians, the Chinese, the Dutch, and even the Greeks, Romans and Barbarians of antiquity.

In a foreshadowing of the Categorical Imperative, Kant notes that feelings of nobility, compassion, and empathy are not virtues in themselves, but rather the submission to a transcendent purpose makes one virtuous.

To Kant, there is a psychic shift that must take place in the individual to engage the beautiful and the sublime. The inability to experience or consume beauty as a limited sensual leads the virtuous soul to transcend the limited state to a moral being capable of entering into the sublime. This Spiritual-Moral psychic faculty within the soul must be awakened by the denial of the sensual, not a relinquishing of the consciousness to the absurdity of emotional, sensual experience of the kinetic universe.

Swedenbough & Synchronicity

Kant's initial application of a skeptical method, characterized by the demonstration of propositions and their opposites, was not limited to establishing a doctrine of doubt, but aimed at exposing the illusions of anti-Metaphysical Reason. This methodology, evident in his earlier work "Dreams of a Spirit-Seer", was crucial to the development of his metaphysical ideas. Kant's 1766 "Träume eines Geistersehers, erläutert durch Träume der Metaphysik" is directed towards the "charlatan" metaphysicians of his day, using Swedenborg's claims of spirit-visions as the central example. It is a cynical, scathing, and mocking criticism of Swedenborgian metaphysics, while simultaneously undermining the faulty Epistemology of Leibniz. Kant addresses "Mr. Schwedenberg" directly and analyzes his works methodically. This is one of his most obscure manuscript, and for good reasons. It is a winding work which pulls the reader into multiple directions and was criticized by Kant himself. Even here in a small, anonymous early work, Kant is laying the foundation of his title of the "Newton of Morals", splitting reality into two subdivisions between Form and Sense-Perception; an ontological divide between a Numinal and Phenomenological world. He creates a broader vision of Swedenborg's cosmological worldview and deconstructs it as ridiculous according to Enlightenment rationality, and even worse, immoral. He manages to make his critique of Swedenborg's anti-Humic in his statement that a real image of Metaphysics relies on living a moral life. Without this, there is no transcendent realities to be experienced.

More broadly, he is sketching out the left and right delineators in his response to the Aristotelian metaphysics of Hume while trying to upload the Scientific advances of the Enlightenment. He uses Occam's Razor against Swedenborg, using pure Enlightenment reason to deconstruct his claims which at points sounds Humic. But at the same time, he begins to back against a pure Newtonian mechanical, deterministic worldview: "For in the relations of cause and effect, of substance and action, philosophy serves at first to resolve the intricate phenomena and to bring such to simpler conceptions." It is certainly his least anti-Enlightenment out of all of his works.

Emanuel Swedenborg was not a mere charlatan spiritualist. He was a dedicated scientist for many years, ran a scientific publication, and was an important advisor on geometry, chemistry, and metallurgy to the royal family of Sweden. He was the first know scientist to understand the concept of Neurons in the brain and charted the first ideals of Synaptic relays. His anatomical and physiological studies were decades ahead of his time. Much later in life, in his 50's, he began to have dreams and visions. He recorded these in dream journals. Later in life, he dedicated himself entirely to Biblical and Theological studies but strayed from Christian Orthodoxy into heavily mystical, spiritualist, and pluralistic lines of thought. He developed an entire theory of the relationship between the material and spiritual world and saw no conflict between believing in both.

Kant did not immediately discount Swedenborg's clairvoyant claims. He acquired Swedenborg's entire enigmatic *Arcana Cælestia* (Heavenly Arcana or Heavenly Mysteries) and studied the whole thing before we have any record of his opinions. Written in Latin, *Arcana Cælestia* is an inaccessible exegesis of scripture and a defense of his metaphysical view of Correspondence, or "simultaneous" levels of existence. Swedenborg claimed that this whole idea was revealed to him, in a similar fashion to Kant's claim that absolute morality is a factor of common sense, not a unique idea of his. Kant considered Swedenborg a serious scholar and academic, which might be why he published this criticism of his theories anonymously. Kant himself did not hold his Dreams of a Spirit-Seer in high esteem and criticized his own arguments against Swedenborg in his correspondence with Moses Mendelssohn years later. Perhaps this is why this work is nearly entirely unknown- it is sloppy and an immature version of Kant's dialectics.

Throughout Carl Jung's philosophic substructure of Analytic Psychology, he used Kant's dichotomy of the Neo-Platonic subdivision of the Numinal and Phenomenological world to support his mystical-scientific concept of Synchronicity, which Swedenborg's Correspondence theory is a shoddy echo, and specifically cites Dreams of a Spirit-Seer:

The effective (numinous) agents in the unconscious are the archetypes. By far the greatest number of spontaneous synchronistic phenomena that I have had occasion to observe and analyze can easily be shown to have a direct connection with an archetype. This, in itself, is an irrepressible, psychoid factor… when, for instance, the vision arose in Swedenborg's mind of a fire in Stockholm, there was a real fire raging there at the same time, without there being any demonstrable or even thinkable connection between the two… we must assume that there was a lowing of the threshold of consciousness which gave him access to "absolute knowledge". The fire in Stockholm was, in a sense, burning in him too. For the unconscious psyche space and time seem to be relative; that is to say, knowledge finds itself in a space-time continuum in which space is no longer space, not time time.

In is 1770 Latin defense, he distinguishes between the Real use of concepts and the Logical use of concepts. The Real is very platonic in nature, while the "The logical use of understanding is common to all sciences, whereas the real use is not". Science, then, Kant wrestles into a narrow but important Epistemological category. The most real types of knowledge are outside of objective Phenomenon. This is a reconciliation of both Plato and Aristotle.

We can see how Jung is combining Hegel and Kant with the idea of "absolute knowledge" and the dichotomy of the Numinal and Phenomenological. Kant was the first recorded philosopher (pre-dating newton by just a couple years) in his statement that gravity can act at a distance, foreshadowing Quantum Entanglement and Jungian-Einsteinian iteration of Panpsychist this experiment resurrected. There is an oceanic tautology between Kant and Jung's psychology in relation to the sophistry of Subject-Object perception. Jung misunderstands Kant's criticism of the event as evidence for it: "This case is well authenticated. See report in Kant's Dreams of a Spirit seer" even though the entire point of this work is to discredit the whole idea of interaction with a spirit world directly. Jungian philosophy is heavily influenced by German Idealism, and continued Kant's work of making religious beliefs acceptable to a materialistic metaphysic.

However, both Kant, Hegel and Jung all articulate at different points that Rationalizing faith is a foolhardy attempt as the human psyche does not ultimately operate on presuppositional rational axoims, but Symbolism. Kant speaks of Archetypes guiding the pneumatic world long before Jung did:

The soul's world is not a world of spirits, but a world of archetypes, which are accompanying ideas of those of the other world, and therefore, what I think as a spirit is not remembered by me as a human being, and vice versa, my state as a human being does not come into the idea of myself as a spirit at all

Ultimately, Kant sees these questions of synchronicity, spiritualism and mysticism broadly (eventually he would include simple prayer in this category, which would get him in trouble with the Lutheran church) as useless to the primary task of human life, which is to live moral lives according to God's Rational purpose:

Let us therefore leave to speculation and to the care of idle minds all noisy doctrinal statements of such remote objects.... They are, in fact, indifferent to us, and the momentary appearance of reasons for or against may perhaps decide the applause of the schools, but hardly anything about the future fate of the righteous.

After writing about the paralogisms of Swedishborgianism from an Empiricist perspective in his 1766 *Träume eines Geistersehers, erläutert durch Träume der Metaphysik,* Kant turned towards more heavy criticism of the works of David Hume. The Prolegomena was published two years after the first edition of the Critique of Pure Reason and summarizes the Critique's essential arguments utilizing phraseology and lines of thought not present in the first edition. This was intended by Kant as a simplified and clear presentation of the Critique, and he would later work some of these summaries back into later versions of the Critique. It is a hostile polemic against the Empiricism of Deterministic Causality and charts an Ontotheology based on human understanding itself. Here he returns to the basic ideas of his Metaphysics and lays the foundation for a Metaphysical science that is as respected as mathematics or physics.

Kant is very clear here that it is David Hume's philosophy which is "exactly that which first interrupted my dogmatic slumber many years ago and gave my investigations in the field of speculative philosophy a completely different direction". We have here an abridged version of Transcendental Dialects against Hume's dialectic of pure reason which sees causal relationships as subjective-psychological realities. All these metaphysics drive toward the dismantling of morality as mere feelings, not absolute realities.

Just like the Critique, the Prolegomena is Epistemological in nature, focusing on questions on the perception and acquisition of knowledge. Kant muses on a range of Cosmological and Noetic questions, such as how are a priori assumptions possible, or how is knowledge from pure reason possible? How is our noumenal consciousness structured, and how does it "know" the world"? What are Space, time, and the cosmos, and how does God interact with or is known by the material world and its inhabitants?

Absolute Knowledge and Subjective Empiricism

Kant's Latin dissertation of 1770 'De mundi sensibilis atque intelligibilis forma et principiis' was a requirement for a professorship at the University of Königsberg, but it outlines his entire worldview, particularly the fundamental Numerical-Platonic split fully fleshed out in the "Critique of Pure Reason". Appointed professor at Königsberg, Kant defended his dissertation in 1770. Despite his reservations about the execution of the dissertation, Kant saw value in three of its five sections, as he revealed in a correspondence with Lambert on 2 September 1770. He expressed dissatisfaction with its initial form, but recognized its fundamental role in his later, more comprehensive work. This later work, outlined in a letter first to Marcus Herz on 7 June 1771, eventually evolved into the seminal Critique of Pure Reason, published in 1781.

The content of Kant's dissertation, particularly sections two and three, which found their way into the Critique of Pure Reason, is primarily concerned with transcendental aesthetics. However, in his 1770 letter to Lambert, Kant indicated the lesser importance of sections one and four of the dissertation. The remaining content, particularly from section five, touches on aspects that would later be addressed in the Transcendental Doctrine of Judgement within the Critique. This progression from a 'dogmatic' theory of pure understanding and reason in the dissertation to a more critical perspective in the Critique underlines a significant development in Kant's thought.

In his letter to Marcus Herz of 21 February 1772, Kant openly discussed the obstacles he encountered in conceptualising the theoretical part of a work entitled "The Limits of Sensation and Reason". He realized that he had omitted a crucial aspect which would later form the core mystery of his metaphysics in the "Critique of Pure Reason". This aspect concerns the relationship of pure concepts of understanding to an object, a revelation that significantly altered his philosophical trajectory. Kant himself, in his post-publication correspondence, notably with Marcus Herz on 1 May 1781 and Johann Bernoulli on 16 November 1781, was more cautious about linking the dissertation to his later work. He acknowledged the fundamental role of the dissertation in his intellectual journey, but also noted the emergence of new, unforeseen challenges in understanding the intellectuality of our cognition, which significantly influenced the development of his later work. This classing of Newtonian mechanics and Cartesian individuality follows him throughout his entire philosophic project.

Published one year before the Critique of Pure Reasons, Metaphysical Foundations is Kant's methodology which would be used in his famous Critique. He attempts to deconstruct an Empiricist Epistemology and show that a priori principles, which are inherently metaphysical in nature, are necessary for the possibility of science to happen in the first place. He is reconciling the new mechanical causality concepts created by Newton with their philosophic preconceptions. While his theory of Phoronomy and movement are not useful to modern physics, this work outlines some basic Epistemological Platonic criticisms of Material Determinism which would be proven Empirically, ironically, by Einstein's Quantum theories and modern theories of perceptual consciousness. One of the most fascinating contributions Kant brings to modern Science is in Quantum theory. Kant, not Newton or Einstein, was the first to posit the theory of "action at a distance" which would eventually be proven by the observation of Quantum Entanglement. In the second section of this treaty, he writes Theorem 7 as "The attraction essential to all matter is a direct effect of the same on others through empty space".

The Metaphysical Foundations is an exploration of the a priori assumptions underlying the study and application of the Physical Science. Kant had great reverence for Newton as a scientist, and never questioned the scientific developments of the Newtonian Enlightenment. But here he explores four assumptions which enable humanity to even practice Physics in the first place. First, he understands the movement of objects being a quantity within Phoronomy. The second section concerns attraction as the force of gravity in space fulfilment. This is a treatise on gravity where he makes a small claim that the force of attraction is independent of distance, a bizarre claim which would be proven correct by modern Quantum Mechanics. In the third section, Kant follows basic Newtonian Mechanics, and in the fourth section he outlines the origins of knowledge, which is Phenomenological, not scientific, in nature.

Kant considered Physics to be a "pure" science, a view which is still common today. Kant and other enlightenment thinkers saw Newtonian Physics as the realization of the "Mathesis universalis", a hypothetical universal science founded on mathematics. Both Descartes and Leibniz, among with many other 16th and 17th-century philosophers supported this model. Kant writes in one of his early models of his Metaphysical system: "I know that there are many who find worldly wisdom very easy in comparison with higher mathesis. But they call everything worldly wisdom that is written in the books that bear this title."

Kant is trying to untangle this Gordian Knot and prevent Newtonian Mechanics from taking this mantle of Mathesis Universalis and becoming the sole causal factor to explain all reality. He writes that the Empiricists "mix up the boundaries of the sciences and sometimes want to philosophize in the theory of quantities, which is why they still try to explain such concepts, although the definition in such a case has no mathematical consequence".

Hegel wrote in his Encyclopedia "Among other things, Kant has the merit to have made the beginning of a concept of matter by his attempt of a so-called construction of matter in his Metaphysical Beginning of Natural Science and to have reawakened the concept of a natural philosophy with this attempt."

Kant's 1788 *Critique of Practical Reason* is the second of his major triad of critical philosophic critiques. It builds upon his *Pure Reason* and the *Groundwork for the Metaphysics of Morals* in delineating his theory of moral justification. The Critique of Pure Reason answers the question, "What can I know?", while Practical Reason answers "what should I do?". Practical Reason primarily concerns the relationship of Reason to morality. It is the "Imperative" in the "Categorical Imperative. He deconstructs and disregards the Empiricist approach of the English philosophers, primarily Hume, as well as the weak Christian argument used by Christian principalities in the Middle Ages that morality is merely the Will of God, in addition to the vague idea that Happiness is the highest good or most moral action. He uses the violent history of Europe, particularly the Divine Right to rule, as an example of the danger of Hume's Heteronomy, which he considers equally dangerous. Morality is not a feeling or perception, but a reality to submit to.

Kant's approach to reason is fundamentally in contrast to the English Empiricist view. His German critical view is a teleological construction of reason which is normative and descriptive. Hume, Locke, and Descartes' view is that "Reason is the slave of the passions" and can tell us nothing about morality and ethics. The teleological view, which is found clearly and explicitly in Kant and all German Idealists after him, is both normative and descriptive, or in other words, Imperative. The entire Frankfurt school of thought operates off of a version of this metaphysical view, all the way to Adorno's Aesthetics which is rooted in a Teleological view of reason. Here Kant clearly breaks out the competing moral theories and their relationship to reason, which he views as exhaustive. The subjective categories of External determinants (Education and Civil Constitution) and Internal (Physical Feelings and moral feelings). He places Stoic philosophy and the Theological moralists in a second category of "Objective", which is better, but still not correctly Categorical. He again defends the finality of the Kantian Categorical Imperative, which he understands as intuitively knowable by all rational agents. Stoicism is an honorable philosophy, but Kant argues it is still not Transcendental or based on a priori, teleological Reason. This law of practical reason, of Categorical morality, he defines here as "Act in such a way that the maxim of your will can at the same time be regarded as the principle of a general legislation."

He writes in the Critique of Pure Reason a foreshadowing of this work:

As far as practical reason is entitled to lead us, we shall not look upon the actions as obligatory because they are the commands of God, but look upon them as divine commands because we have an inner obligation to follow them. We shall study freedom in view of the purposive unity in accordance with the principles of reason, and we shall believe ourselves to be acting in accordance with the divine will only insofar as we hold sacred the moral law which reason teaches us from the nature of actions themselves. We shall believe ourselves to be serving this will only by promoting, both in ourselves and in others, everything that is best in the world. Moral theology is, therefore, only of immanent use. It enables us to fulfill our destination here in the world by adapting ourselves to the system of all ends, without either fanatically or even criminally abandoning the hiding thread of a morally legislative reason in the proper conduct of our lives, but in order to connect this thread directly with the idea of the highest being... As, then, the moral precept is at the same time my maxim (reason commanding that it should be so), I shall inevitably believe in the existence of God and in a future life and I feel certain that nothing can shake this belief because all my moral principles would be overthrown at the same time and I cannot surrender them without becoming hateful in my own eyes.

In Practical Reason, he meditates further on the Highest Good throughout the text. The a priori pure unconditional ideas of God, Immortality of the soul, and Freedom preceded the ability to Reason in the first place, so they cannot be proven in Externality, as Medieval Catholic Cosmotheology espouses, but only as postulates of pure practical reason, known through the rationality of the soul. This is a continuum of contra-Enlightenment thought which extends to Hegel who builds it out further, known as Ontotheology.

Freedom is still central to Kant's entire philosophic project, and the Humean doctrine of Heteronomy receives more wrath in this work. Kant writes that Autonomy, true human freedom to act independent of mechanical causality, is a universal principle of all moral law, but this autonomy necessitates duty to an abstract principle: "The autonomy of the will is the sole principle of all moral laws and the duties that correspond to them: All heteronomy of the will, on the other hand, not only does not establish any obligation at all but is rather contrary to the principle of it and the morality of the will."

"Herewith I end my whole critical business" Kant states in the preface to his third and final Critique in his core triad of critical philosophic treatises. In his old age, he turned from being Polemic to being prescriptive in his vision for a future of transcendental, rational morality. Here he recaps his whole critical system and breaks out his final thoughts between a Critique of Aesthetic Judgment and the Critique of Teleological Judgment. Between Pure Reason (theoretical) and Practical Reason (law and ethics) stands the mediating Power of Judgement which recognizes the particular in the general and bridges the chasm between sensuality and morality, nature and freedom, manifesting itself to the senses. To that end, he sees beauty as a critical, supersensuous bridge between the Subject and Object, a reflective dialectic that unites this Platonic divide between Numina and Phenomena. The field of Aesthetics seems to be a niche field to identify as the lynchpin of his entire dialectal, Teleological rational morality , but to Kant the correct recognition of what beauty is, and responding to it authentically (morally), is vital to his entire project.

Kant's Teleological, dialectal understanding of the experience of art is still used today in Modern art theory. Namely, his analysis of sublimity as "disinterested pleasure" as an aesthetic experience between the dynamics of the cognitive faculties of sensuality and rationality, creates a paradox of judgment as both subjective and universal.

Hegel based his Lectures on Aesthetics on these Kantian categories and the correlation between consciousness and noumenon. To Hegel, the sensuous, aesthetic experience of beauty, when properly understood, leads us to the supersensuous experience of consciousness. Art is the expression of the Idea; it reflects the "pure

I's" understanding of itself. Art is pragmatic; beauty is pragmatic- it develops the Subject's self-consciousness and corrects its metaphysical relationship to the Object. To Kant and Hegel, Beauty is realized through the particularization of the Universal, and the highest form of this paradox is the divine. Art is instantiating the General in the specific to Hegel as much as it is to Kant. Goethe and Shiller, Hegel muses, was a genius in his storytelling precisely because he understood this- because he "narrowly limited particularity from the life of the present, but at the same time, as a background and as the atmosphere in which this circle moves... the broadest, most powerful world events." This contrast generates sublimity, and genius creates sublime art because they are attuned to nature. Kant gives a nearly identical explanation: " Sublimity is not contained in anything of nature, but only in our mind, insofar as we can become conscious of being superior to nature in us, and thereby also to nature (insofar as it flows into us) outside of us. Everything that arouses this feeling in us, to which belongs the power of nature, which calls upon our forces, is then called (although not really) sublime; and only on the condition of this idea in us, and relation to it, are we able to arrive at the idea of the sublimity of that being, which not only by its power, which it demonstrates in nature, works intimate respect in us, but even more by the capacity, which is placed in us, to judge it without fear, and to think of our destiny as superior to it."

The 'Dasein' of the individual experiences Beauty in Kanto-Hegelian Aesthetics. Dasein, the Ontologic Being of personal reality, is a purely philosophic concept of Being which maintains within itself an antinomy of finitude-infinity. Hegel defines Dasein in his Encyclopedia as "the unity of being and nothing in which the immediacy of these determinations and thus their contradiction in their relationship has disappeared - a unity in which they are only moments". Self-Consciousness, or Dasein, experiences itself through beauty: "Now when truth in this external existence [Dasein] is present to consciousness immediately, and with the concept remains immediately in unity with its external appearance, the Idea is not only true but beautiful. Beauty is determined as the sensible shining of the Idea."

Kant foreshadows Hegel in understanding the Teleological nature of Reason and Geist: "Spirit, in the aesthetic sense, means the animating principle in the mind. But that by which this principle enlivens the soul, the substance it uses for this purpose, is that which purposefully sets the forces of the mind in motion, i.e., in such a play that sustains itself and itself strengthens the forces for this purpose."

The core and enigmatic base reality of human consciousness, which Kant calls "Transcendental Apperception", is without known origin, he argues. Existing parallel, separate from yet within this Transcendent self-consciousness are the rules for the knowledge of all things (Categories) built in prior to any sensory experience or external logic being obtained. It cannot be subject to even Transcendental deduction; there is simply no foundation to investigate its origin or nature. Here he comes very near to describing a soul but avoids using religious or outright Idealist language. As Kant's fellow German Dietrich Bonhoeffer (a budding Kantian philosopher prior to his untimely demise) put his Categorical Imperative "People have eyes to see; they bear within themselves the potential to arrive at the eternal essentials."

The 'Manifold' in Kant's philosophy is the indeterminate multiplicity and sequence of sensory contents. The categories needed to sort this chaotic contact with the material reality we find ourselves enveloped by cannot be arrived at by Empiricism alone; rather, they must exist independent of experience from the profound unconscious phenomenological depths of the human mind. Kant has never been described as an Existentialist, but he does almost describe a type of Thrownness in that he describes the human soul as "enfolded by nature with limits that can never be altered". Fidelity to this unalterable reality of human consciousness is necessary to build any coherent and universally applicable Metaphysics.

Schopenhauer believed that "The Critique of Pure Reason transformed ontology into dianoiology." Hegel developed Kant's philosophy further, but where he regressed, in Dostoevskian terms, is by arguing that the soul can be fully understood as it is perfectly rational. Kant denies this because it is "enfolded by nature with limits that can never be altered" and thus, the transcendental "I" can never be known by itself. The psychic reality that the neurologic of humans operates off symbolic thought, narrative not presuppositions, is nearly apodictic today.

Here in the Critique of Judgement, Kant does not approach Aesthetics in a Temporal-Spatial and Transcendental manner as he does in the Critique of Pure Reason, but primarily as the theory of sensory perception. To Kant, Aesthetics is a dynamic interplay of sensual perception and Teleological natural categories, so they rely on the a priori principles used to perceive through the manifold of sensory experience. He does not emphasize a priori knowledge here but focuses on the interaction of objective knowledge and subjective judgments. This is done to focus on the practical ethics needed by society:

> I will proceed unhesitatingly to the doctrinal, in order, where possible, to gain from my increasing age the still somewhat favorable time for it. It is self-evident that there is no special part for the power of judgment in it because, concerning it, criticism serves instead of theory; but after the division of philosophy into the theoretical and practical, and the pure, into just such parts, the metaphysics of nature and that of morals will make up that business.

And these morals which are the crux of his whole philosophical undertaking beginning with his reaction to Hume manifest themselves as Faith:

> Faith (as a habitus, not as an actus) is the moral way of thinking of reason in believing that which is inaccessible to theoretical knowledge. It is therefore the persistent principle of the mind, that which is a condition for the possibility of the highest moral end.

In contrast to the concept of Reason used by the English Empiricists, and subsequently, the Analytic Philosophers, the Metaphysician of Königsberg posits a fundamentally different view of reason as inherently Teleological and thus Universal, laying the foundation of Continental Philosophy. Kant is answering David Hume's ethics, an epicurean iteration that taught that what is moral is that which is good for yourself. It's a purely subjective morality depending on one's own opinion. Kant spent 11 years of his life systematically reading and analyzing the "cold-blooded David Hume" and responds here in his most well-rounded work. He is broadly reproaching the Newtonian mechanical reductionist in the tradition of the English Empiricists and their view that "Reason is the slave of the passions", but also reproaching the reactions to this materialism including Platonic Idealism. Kant's friction with Hume is an echo of the debates between the Skeptics and the Platonists, specifically, and today's Functionalist versus Structuralist Anthropology is a reconstruction of the conflict between Hume and Kant. The German idealists as the core of modern Philosophy, while Hegel and Kant are clear that it's all been downhill from Plato.

Reason to Kant is both the means and the ends, while Reason to the Empiricists is solely the means. David Hume's fundamental error in Kant's view is that he assumes a Rationality which is Techne without Telos, a description only of what is, not what should be. To this end, he uses a Greek conception of Rationality as logos within a Platonic Ontology, splitting reality into two subdivisions between form and sense- perception, between Numinal and a phenomenological world. As physics is pure science, metaphysics is pure philosophy; "Pure knowledge of reason from mere concepts is called pure philosophy, or metaphysics... Metaphysics, then, both of nature and of morals, and especially the critique of reason venturing out on its own wings, which precedes it in a propaedeutic way, are actually the only things that we can call philosophy in the true sense of the word".

Metaphysics is not optional, for all action presupposes embedded metaphysical ethics: "Natural science, which can actually be called this, first presupposes metaphysics of nature; for laws, i.e. principles of the necessity of what belongs to the existence of a thing, deal with a concept that cannot be constructed because existence cannot be represented a priori in any view. Therefore real natural science presupposes metaphysics of nature."

The Critique lays the foundation of his Systematic Metaphysics published across a dozen works with the singular aim of 'fixing' the field by reconciling Rationalism, Idealism, and Empiricism to move Metaphysics into a full form of Science, much, in the same manner, the Greeks did to Logic or The Renaissance logicians to the hard sciences. Kant sparked a metaphysical revolution which he understands as akin to the Copernican revolution. The question of how the iterations of the transcendent 'I' through time and space can 'know' anything (make synthetic a priori judgments) with any level of certainty takes the proscenium in the Critique. Kant's critical philosophy is intricately architectonically woven propositional reasoning divided and subdivided into their elements all the way down into rudimentary Phenomenological and Epistemological assumptions. It does not erase but rather restrains and builds upon Idealist and Empiricist terminology while creating a new lexicon necessary to express his Transcendental Idealism. At the center of his Transcendental Apperception of the human consciousness is a nascent Existential Thrownness; he writes that the enigmatic core of consciousness (preceding the Manifold of sensory perception) is "enfolded by nature with limits that can never be altered".

Kant makes it clear that Transcendental Idealism does not rely on mere deduction, but on argumentation from a range of evidence much like a legal argument. Some of his arguments are apagogical and he is clear when the topic demands such a type of logic. A priori beliefs are only possible through the synthesis of the Manifold, not through Empiricism or Rationalism. He writes: "For without intuition, all our knowledge is without objects, and therefore remains entirely empty. For no truth can contradict it without losing at the same time all content, that is, all related to any object." IV OF the Division of Transcendental Logic into Transcendental Analytic and Dialectic" and later "Knowledge is first produced by the synthesis of a manifold" (Section 10 Of the Pure Concepts of the Understanding or Categories). His Transcendental Aesthetic lays out the Science of the principles of a priori sensibility and in the Analytic of Principles, Kant sets to distinguishing Phenomena and Noumena (between the perception of things and the objective reality of things.

The very act of interacting with the world presupposes an ethic; an embedded religion and Kant argues that acknowledgment of pure consciousness, a Transcendental "I", is the starting point of knowing oneself. But, contrary to Hegel, he argues that one can never truly understand oneself, only the image of oneself, just as one can only know the existence of, but not the essence of objects in the universe. He writes about this 'icon' of the self we can experience:

This [Figurative Synthesis] we can always perceive in ourselves. We cannot think of a line without drawing it in thought; we cannot think of a circle without describing it; we cannot represent, at all, the three dimensions of space without placing, from the same point, three lines perpendicularly to one another... merely to the act of the synthesis of the manifold whereby we successively determine the inner sense, and thereby to the succession of this determination in an inner sense... I have no knowledge of myself as I am but only as I appear to myself. The Consciousness of oneself is therefore very far from being knowledge of oneself

The contradiction Kant admits and attempts to solve is the unknowability of the Thing-in-and-of-itself, a truly independent external world. Noumenon exists, although we cannot "know" them. Hegel would disagree, and plot a course to the knowability of external objects. Kant held the view that we can know they exist, just not know them directly, and that worldly objects can be intuited a priori ('beforehand'). Intuition is therefore independent of objective reality. To Kant, these are knowable to God, but unknowable to the limited material mind through the a priori forms, which are the mediation between Being and the external world. Being and negation are two of these a priori forms. But how can we know what these external realities are if the External world is unknowable to the Self? Kant avoids denying the Thing-in-an-of-itself because then all reality would be merely Mind, with creates both form and content. How are synthetic propositions a priori possible?

Kant defines a priori as "a knowledge that is independent of experience and even of all impressions of the senses" and a posteriori as the knowledge that derives from experience, i.e. Empirical knowledge. First and foremost in his Epistemology is the question: "How are synthetic a priori propositions possible? If in an a priori judgment we want to go beyond the given concept, we find that which can both be discovered a priori and be synthetically connected with it, not in the concept, but in the intuition corresponding to that concept. For this reason, however, such judgments can never reach beyond objects of the senses, and are valid only for objects of possible experience."

His ideology here is a critical philosophy that delineates the boundaries of human knowledge and isn't true idealism yet. The German Idealists built upon this Kantian foundation but expanded the Subject to the collective, to the Geist, a move which Kant initiated. Kant is beginning to move towards a Collective Subject, deeply linked to the Categorical Imperative, which binds all people together in one. Kant does not go as far as to say there is a unified Psychic substratum between all people, or that the Archetypes reside there, as Hegel and Jung would posit, but he does make the shift towards an Oceanic view of humanity as one collective Geist. The mind is anything to the German Idealists but a Tabula Raza.

And here is the 'Transcendental' and the mystical element; there is a reality, the third type of knowledge which allows Idealism and Empiricism to exist at all, that envelops us and exists in an ontological and epistemological different sphere altogether. Our chaotic subconscious intuitions (the dynamic Manifold of sensory knowledge) are shaped into our individual reality of experience, our consciousness, through the a priori and a posteriori categories of knowledge, what Kant calls the Synthesis. It is at this Synthesis that we can communicate and commune with other humans; this is the unifying 'platform' of our existence, what enables us to hold truths and knowledge in common as a collection of individuals. These Categories exist independent of sensory experience and cannot be derived from any Empirical logic or reasoning. He writes: "Rationalism only leads to an elaborate illusion of knowledge;

Empiricism can take us further to know the existence of things, but we can never know the true nature of things."

Dietrich Bonhoeffer wrote in his 1929 Act and Being (a Ph.D. thesis later published) "it is never possible for a systematic metaphysics to know that once 'cannot give oneself truth' for such knowledge would already signify a placing oneself into truth...If 'it' were in the truth of the divine word it could not celebrate the triumph of the I, of the spirit, but would have to recognize in its eternal loneliness the curse of lost community with God [Gottesgemeinschaft]. Only a way of thinking that, bound in obedience to Christ, 'is' from the truth can place into the truth... we need to see that [revelation] as a step that must already have been taken so that we may be able to take it at all"

Consciousness is ontologically bound to these Categories; they can only exist because the inherent nature of the consciousness of the individual allows them to and vice versa. Certain "pure" concepts exist as part of our very existence and allow a priori knowledge to exist; "The mere but empirically determined, consciousness of my own existence proves the existence of objects in space outside myself."

The demand of having an imperative universal to all humans necessitates that all humans have a common experience or psychic state. The individual has a personal duty that is passionately individualistic and existentialist, but also stands with all humans through all time; the individual is One consciousness. This universal Consciousness is central to his argument that Morality can be known by all people individually from their innate rationality. Without this, there can be no shared moral principles. Even in his dialectics on the physical nature of reality, he writes "Everything in the universe has a relation to everything else". Kant begins the path towards this Pansychism here but does not complete this loop in the absence of Psychology as a field of science. This move towards the universalization of the Mind solves the Idealistic Solipsism which Hegel accuses Kant of. Fichte, Schelling, and finally Hegel broke up the hegemony of Kantian philosophy and moved it forward by fixing an Epistemological contradiction and fixing the problem of the knowability of the External world through collectivizing consciousness with a temporal dynamism with an ultimate purpose, a Teleology, to history and Mind.

Kanto-Hegelian Ontotheology: Christianity as Phaenomena

and Noumena for the Masses

Even today, there is confusion between Platonic Idealism and the basic divide of Platonic Ontology. There are rationalistic Protestants who misunderstand Platonic Ontology as meaning the physical world does not exist outside of the idea of it, conflating Platonic Idealism with the Platonic Ontology upon which Christianity was built. This Platonic split between form and content, phaenomena and noumena, is the metaphysical principle clashing with Enlightenment, Materialistic One-World Rationalism. Kant is condemning the specific Cosmology of Platonic Idealism but splits the world into two co-dependent realities just like Plato does.

Kant specifically takes aim at Platonic Idealism; the idea that objects only exist as our representations and subsequently, he laughs off the arguments of Anselm, Aquinas, and other Western logisticians for their partial reliance on this type of logic. Phenomenologically, Platonic idealism is holds water, but in Newtonian-inspired rationalism, it has no place. Kant is trying to reconcile Empirical and Skeptical forms of thought to metaphysical thinking. There are elements of the medieval satire of Rubens and Erasmus throughout Kant's works. Kant is not so much criticizing Religion writ large as he is criticizing poorly Platonized religion and the interpretation of Aristotle (misinterpretation in Hegel's reading); that revelation without mysticism is broken, incomplete and ultimately derivative. His Transcendental Dialectic is dedicated to criticizing Rational Morality as much as it criticizes Rational Theology. In this, he is broadly Platonic, but utilizing anti-platonic rationality to try to establish the Platonic a priori forms. Heidegger wrote:

Then Aristotle was no less an idealist than Kant. If idealism means tracing everything that exists back to a subject or consciousness, which are only characterized by the fact that they remain indeterminate in their being and are at most negatively characterized as "undetermined", then this idealism is methodologically no less naïve than the crudest realism.

The analysis of space is still subordinate here. Although the dialectic is already breaking through, it does not yet have the later rigid, schematic form, but still enables a loosened understanding of the phenomena. On the path from Kant to Hegel's fully developed system, Aristotelian ontology and logic once again make a decisive incursion. This has long been known as a fact.

Even as a Christian moralist, Kant takes aim at the dominant arguments that Protestants and Catholics used to argue against One-World Aristotelian Naturalism. He systematically deconstructs the hundreds of thousands of Cosmological, Ontologic, and Teleological (physico-theological) arguments of the scholastics, particularly Anselm's Proslogium, and declares them all as untenable, and even dangerous as they are inadvertently establishing the same faulty metaphysics that atheistic rationality is founded upon. He posits a more nuanced Ontotheological apologetic based on metaphysical a priori realities. He writes:

Accordingly, I maintain that the physico-theological proof can never alone demonstrate the existence of a supreme being, but must at all times leave it to the ontological proof (which it serves only for an introduction) to supplement this deficiency so that the latter still contains the only possible reason for proof (insofar as only a speculative proof takes place everywhere), which no human reason can bypass.

He is attempting here to sort out the chaff and start over, as these arguments have done nothing to convince the Empiricists, and Western society simply continued to secularize, despite the rabid intellectualism of self-made Cosmologists trying to "prove" the existence of God. To Kant, God is an Idea (a pure, elemental concept generated by Reason) that cannot be confirmed experientially nor denied. Rather, the idea of God has a regulatory function that does not further our knowledge per se, but rather lays the foundation of knowledge itself; a metaphysical ability to give the individual a pure form of knowledge and motivation to seek knowledge in the first place. He indirectly states that the faulty foundation the West has created is the problem, and this must be put right through a Platonic Ontology, otherwise all apologetics is folly unless the soul understands its reality correctly: "But the mere doctrinal faith has something shaky in it; one is often put out of it by difficulties that are found in speculation, although one inevitably returns to it again and again... The trick of the cosmological proof aims only at avoiding the proof of the existence of a necessary being a priori by mere concepts, which would have to be carried out ontologically, but which we feel completely incapable of doing."
He levels the same argument against the Skeptics, Epicureans, and Empiricists of his day, arguing that Reason cannot assert truth beyond Empirical observation, I.e. sensory experience, and that using

this type of knowledge alone to draw larger conclusions is zealotry and dogma, not critical thinking. Kant writes in the preface to the Second Edition: "For the dogmatism of metaphysics, that is, the presumption that it is possible to achieve anything in metaphysics without a preceding critique of pure reason, is the source of all that disbelief which opposes morality and which is always very dogmatic." While Kant rejected Divine Command & Natural Law theory, he did not assert the naturally opposite and popular idea of his time that Theology is not needed for morality, or in other words that morals can be ascertained through Reason alone (Empiricism). Transcendental Idealism rather keeps the door open (to use a Dostoevskian metaphor) to the supernatural; while Reason is critical and central to developing a moral code, it is derived from the same framework that Theism is. Kantian Transcendentalism states that a supra-rational reality is necessary for the creation of Categories by the chaotic manifold of experience processed into shared reality, so in an Epistemological fashion, divinity is a prerequisite for even the possibility of shared morality.

The critical mistake here is that Reason is separate from Theology; rather, to Kant, the belief in the existence of God is itself an "Idea" of pure reason. This was instrumental in making the Arc-Atheist and Trans-Humanist Nietzsche a bitter and passionate Anti-Kantian; he not only allowed for the existence of God but alongside Freedom [Transcendental a priori free will] and the concept of the immortal soul, he believed it is instrumental to a moral society. He writes: "God, freedom, and immortality are not merely regulative ideas that guide our thought in all its quests for knowledge but are concepts that are necessary if truly moral action is to be conceivable at all."

Hegel would develop this line of thought further, utilizing the Neo-Platonic conception of Reason as Logos, that is, Teleological and living. In the Science of Logic, he posits: "Yet Objectivity is just that much richer and higher than the being or existence of the ontological proof, as the pure notion is richer and higher than that metaphysical void of the sum total of all reality. But I reserve for another occasion the more detailed elucidation of the manifold misunderstanding that has been brought by logical formalism into the ontological, as well as the other, so-called proofs of God's existence, as also the Kantian criticisms of them, and by establishing the true significance, to restore the fundamental thoughts of these proofs to their worth and dignity. " (SL § 1533) and in the Phenomenology "The real attestation of the Divinity of Christ is the witness of one's own Spirit- not Miracles; for only Spirit recognizes Spirit.

Subjective-Absolutist Protestant Theology: The Universalization of the Papacy

Kant's 1793 "Religionsschrift" has been one of his more popular books due to its simple nature. This work concerns "the relationship of religion to human nature" and is more Theological and Exegetical in nature than Philosophic. It is inherently Epistemological, as Kant strove to fix both Natural science and Theology by keeping them both in their respective dialectal parameters. Living through the heart of the Enlightenment, Kant observed the Epistemological problems brought about by One-World Newtonian Mechanical Reductionism and the bad counter-reactions that Protestant apologists made. Like Hegel, Kant wants to restore faith as the "guardian of the speculative mysteries". He criticizes the church nearly as much as the Materialistic Rationalist camp.

On a personal level, Kant was raised in a Pietist Lutheran family, and was almost a Deist himself. He was a Christian apologist, but hated organized religion and did not maintain any religious practices himself and was part of no religious community. Salvation, to Kant, is synonymous with living a moral life. He rejects outward spiritual practice, is very anti-Catholic, anti-miracles and any practice which is mystical in nature including, oddly enough, prayer. Some biographers have commented that the simple-minded clergy and theologians of his day were mind-numbingly below Kant's intellect, which developed an understandable disdain for attending church and listing to their drivel. Still, you see a very explicitly Lutheran understanding the Scripture and the use of it, so he did not fall far intellectually from his Lutheran roots. He is very anti-clergy, which is in keeping with the Lutheran Pietist movement which emphasized strongly individualism and oftentimes denounced the need for church entirely.

He holds faith to be extremely individualistic, as a movement of the mind towards a categorical moral standard. Naturally, this cuts out any kind of communal spiritualism or need for a church community and certainly any institution. He uses Luther's metaphysical position of claritas scriptura to establish an even more radical and individualistic version of Sola Scriptura. He defines faith very narrowly as: "Faith (as a habitus, not as an actus) is the moral way of thinking of reason in believing that which is inaccessible to theoretical knowledge. It is therefore the persistent principle of the mind, that which is a condition for the possibility of the highest moral end."

He holds a typical Aristotelian-Medieval Anthropology reminiscent of Augustin's Original Sin, in keeping with Luther, but understands it within his Transcendental Moral framework. For being a Rationalist's Rationalist, he is quote comfortable with mysteries. For example, he holds Divine Election and Free Will as perfectly compatible in a mystical antinomy, in contrast to Luther's heavy emphasis on Predestination and denunciation of the concept of Free Will. He sees the fallen nature of man as the result of libertarian Free Will, a disconnect between the "Moral-legislating World Originator" and the individual's choice to live according to the Imperative.

Dispute of the Faculties is Kant's defense of his religious writings against secular Prussian Lutheran authorities who accused him of a wide range of issues including attempting to wrestle religious power away from Biblical Theologians and corrupting the youth with unbiblical ideas. His *1793 Religion within the Limits of Mere Reason*, his most theological work, cause a stir among the Prussian censorship authorities. The Prussian state still intervened in academic affairs for its own reasons, and Kant's works gained their attention as potentially disruptive. He published only one small lecture on Anthropology after this work before he died.

Merely two years before publishing Dispute of the Faculties, in 1796, Kant wrote a preface for a book titled *About the organ of the soul* by a German scientist named Samuel Thomas Soemmerring, who published works on a range of scientific topics, primarily in anatomy. In it he is wrestling with these same issues, as he was already receiving significant criticism from the government, and was facing his works being censored:

Therefore a responsum is sought over which two faculties can get into arguments because of their jurisdiction [...], the medical, in their anatomical-physiological, with the philosophical, in its psychological-metaphysical subject, where, as with all attempts at a coalition, between those who want to base everything on empirical principles and those who demand a priori reasons... Anyone who, in the present case, thanks the physician as a physiologist will lose it with the philosopher as a metaphysician; and vice versa, whoever pleases him offends against the physiologist

Here and in *Faculties*, he argues for a pragmatic differentiation between the sciences, humanities, theological and philosophic faculties. The Theological faculties should be focused on pragmatic church issues and not conflict with the philosophers. These are practical conflicts that inevitably arise from the Mind-World and Mind-Body paradox.

But the Prussian government was not interested in his high-brow philosophy. The accusations of meddling in state and church affairs came from his *1793 Religion within the Limits of Mere Reason,* which was exclusively a theological systematic on a wide range of issues. His other Apologetics works including his *1763 The Only Possible Ground of Evidence for a Demonstration of the Existence of God* also drew criticism due to his dismissive arguments against the normative cosmological arguments used by the protestant churches of his day.

Hegel faced the exact same problems and repeatably entered into quarrels with the Theologians of his day, who felt that he was stepping on their toes. Hegel received a lot of flak from theologians over his work as they did towards philosophy in general, and in his Lectures on religion, he defends Philosophy writes largely from these detractors:

Even the theologians, who are still only at home when in vanity, have dared to accuse philosophy of its destructive tendency, theologians who no longer possess anything of the substance that could be destroyed... Those who resent philosophy for thinking religion do not know what they are asking... this is the outward appearance of humility, but true humility consists in sinking the mind into truth.

Hegel understands this anti-philosophic bend to be due to the fantasy of Sola Scriptura, a result of Medieval-Catholic Nominalism and Cartesian Epistemology. He was a Protestant Apologist, writing extensively against Catholicism, so his criticism of Sola Scriptura is naturally interesting. Reading it in the context of all of his lectures on Religion over the years, it seems to me to stem from his encounters with Protestant clergy- all of whom thought their interpretation of the Bible is "obvious" and immutable, unable to see that they are interpreting it through the lens of tradition just as much as any Roman Catholic does. Philosophy, then, they attacked because it threatened this illusion- this fantasy of Sola Scriptura- which is the lie their whole Weltbild (worldview) relies upon. Hegel writes

In the Protestant Church, the Bible was the essential basis of the doctrine... it was thought that exegesis, was only to take up the thoughts of the Bible. But in fact, the intellect had established its views, its thoughts, beforehand, and then it was seen how the words of Scripture could be explained according to them... Because this exegesis consults reason, it has come about that a so-called theology of reason has come into being, which is opposed to that doctrinal concept of the church, partly by itself, partly by that which it opposes... the nature of interpretive explanation implies that pre-conceived concepts assert themselves in the process of interpretation... Even in the representation of a philosophical system already developed in itself, e.g. of Plato or Aristotle, it is the case that the representations turn out differently according to the already determined mode of a conception of those who undertake them. From Scripture, therefore, the most opposite opinions have been exegetically proved by theology, and thus this so-called Holy Scripture has been turned into a disguise for heterodoxy. All heresies have invoked the Scriptures.

Kant dances around this exact same issue in the Dispute of the Faculties, while trying to not run afoul of the Lutheran authorities. He writes "a scriptural scholarship of Christianity is subject to many difficulties of the art of interpretation..." Kant and Hegel here are both running into the Tautology created by Luther's Claritas Scriptura, the metaphysical Nominalist foundation of Sola Scriptura, which Luther established from his Augustinian Catholic training in several works and sermons, most notable his 1539 *Über das Studium der Theologie* (About the study of theology) and his 1530 *Ein Sendbrief vom Dolmetschen/* A Letter on Interpretation. Kant and Hegel both dealt with the fallout of these principles in the Enlightenment even after the religious wars of the 16th and 17th centuries.

The Telos of Kant's Rationality in Statecraft

Not to be confused with his much earlier 1785 work *Groundwork for the Metaphysics of Morals* in which he attempts to build a metaphysical foundation for absolute morality, Kant's Metaphysics of Morals focuses on the application of virtue in the real world. In keeping with the grounded, practical themes of his later works, the metaphysician of Prussia's *Die Metaphysik der Sitten* focuses on law, government regulation and virtue. Law is the inevitable end of Reason, and as such, is rooted in *a priori* principles native to the soul but not external experience, in other words, metaphysical. The imperative of virtue relies on internal compulsion, while the imperative of legality relies on an external compulsion. In his lifelong rage against the Empiricism of David Hume, Kant here builds a positive framework devoid of polemics.

The ethical and legal principle to behave in a civil, cosmopolitan manner of mutual respect is an imperative command of Reason, and we are merely acknowledging a theory of law that is intuitive to all rational agents. Kant does not posit that his ideas are new, just clearer than his predecessors. These are the dull, functional manifestations of an Intellectus Arrchytypus native to the whole of humanity. This is the telos of Reason and not merely the Techne- the internal ordering of the soul, the a priori postulates of Reason, tell one not merely how to do something, but what ought to be done. The will is the source of both Morality and Evil. In Kant's Groundwork for the Metaphysics of Morals, he writes:

There is nothing in the world, or even outside of it, that can be considered good without restriction, but only a good will. Understanding, wit, power of judgment, and whatever else the talents of the spirit may be called, or courage, determination, perseverance in resolution as qualities of temperament are undoubtedly good and desirable in some intentions; but they can also become extremely evil and harmful if the will…is not good…. For without principles of good will they can become most evil… The good will is good not by what it brings about or accomplishes, not by its suitability for the attainment of some predetermined end, but solely by the will

Kant's "Doctrine of Rights" explained here would inspire Hegel's 1820 Philosophy of Rights, where he would develop a more robust legal theory and a more restrictive social contract. Kant's legal theory is deeply rooted in his Deontological moral theory which emphasizes duty, what one ought to do, regardless of desire or any other factor. Hegel's theory of governance likewise emphasizes duty, but understands societal advancement more teleologically, creating an entire Eschatology not quite seen in Kant. To Kant, a peaceful world is the telos of Reason, while Hegel sees even beyond world peace. Both see virtue as an elemental choice of the intellectual archetypes of the will.

Kant's 1795 On Perpetual Peace: A Philosophical Draft is one of his most well-known works written in his old age. Here Kant directly applies his Teleological Moral Philosophy he established across his life directly to the field of politics and International Relations. Due to the broken and inherently evil, inherited nature of man, peace is not natural and must be built through adherence to rational maxim on the individual, national and international levels. These binding international laws have built the foundation of anti-Machiavellian

Liberal Internationalism. On Perpetual Peace is one of the foundational philosophic works the international world order, and the charter of the United Nations, was built upon.

The United Nations was founded by Woodrow Wilson, who was a Kantian philosopher, and explicitly used Kant's terminology "league of nations". The imperative under the UN and post-WWII International Relations is inherently Kantian. The Kantian Imperative these "Preliminary Articles" was built upon is inherently Anti-Machiavellian. Kant established the principles that would be enshrined at Westphalia: the non-interference in the internal affairs of another state and that "no state debts shall be incurred in relation to external state dealings". This work as designed to be a template for future agreements between states, hence the reason it is written like a legal contract.

To Kant, world peace is not a philanthropic or sentimental topic, but the inevitable result of the Categorical Imperative, that is, pure a priori reason that is intrinsically Teleological. In the Definitive Article he writes: "The law of nations shall be founded on a federalism of free states... By the malice of human nature... which reveals itself unmistakably in the free relation of nations..."

Kant is the basis of Hegel's Statecraft as he developed a more robust and dogmatic understanding as the State as Reason. His 1820's Elements of the Philosophy of Right attempted "nothing else than an attempt to comprehend and represent the State as something rational in itself." This idea has aged the worst out of all of his philosophical musings. He argues that individual submission to the 'morality of the state' (Sittlichkeit) is the absolute duty of the individual. He called the idea that an individual is responsible to God directly for their moral actions a "peculiarity of the modern time, while the antique morality is based on the principle of abiding by one's duty to the state at large." He even goes as far as attacking Catholicism for maintaining a moral code transcendent of the government's edicts: "The Catholic confession... does not concede to the State an inherent Justice and Morality- a concession which in the Protestant principle is fundamental." This did not age well after Germany in the 1940's.

In his 1797 The Metaphysics of Morals, Kant explains his political theories outlined here even further:

This rational idea of a peaceful, even if not yet friendly, continuous community of all peoples on earth, who can come into effective relations among themselves, is not philanthropic (ethical), but a legal principle. Nature has enclosed them all together (by virtue of the spherical shape of their abode, as globus terraqueus) within certain boundaries; and since the possession of the soil, on which the inhabitant of the earth can live, can always only be thought of as the possession of a part of a certain whole, consequently as such, to which each of them originally has a right: All peoples originally stand in a community of the soil, but not in the legal community of possession (communio) and thus of use or ownership of it, but in the physical possible interaction (commercium), i.e. in a continuous relationship

Kantian Roots of Jungian Archetypes

In several of his works, Kant muses about Christ being the apotheosis of a primordial Archetype, what the founder of Analytic Psychology, Carl Jung, would call the "Archetype of Self-Consciousness" which resides in the Collective Unconscious. He does not consider the biological or genetic factors in the creation of the "supersensous substrate" but gets close:

…the Son of God, if we imagine that divinely minded man, as the archetype for us.. in the appearance of the God-man there is not what comes to mind or can be known through experience, but the archetype lying in our reason, which we subordinate to the latter (because so much can be perceived from his example, being found according to that), actually the object of saving faith, and such faith is one with the principle of a life pleasing to God.

Hegel would go on to call this apotheosis of the Hero Myth archetypically manifest in Christ as a "Uniform Plurality" (Gleichförmige Pluralität). Kant's Moral Teleological apologetic model, which Hegel developed further into a line of thought called Kanto-Hegelian Ontotheology, relies on these intrinsic rational archetypes:

Moral teleology, on the other hand, which is no less firmly founded than physical teleology, but rather deserves preference because it is based a priori on principles inseparable from our reason, leads to what is required for the possibility of a theology, namely, to a definite concept of the supreme cause, as a world cause according to moral laws, consequently to such a cause as satisfies our moral final purpose: for which nothing less than omniscience, omnipotence, omnipresence, etc.

His apologetic model has limits, Kant admits. The Immortality of the Soul, free will and the existence (Dasein) of God are all empirically unprovable but are postulates of Rationality itself. These a priori realities of "pure philosophy, i.e. Metaphysics, are necessary for Reason and the application of Reason to the material work, i.e. science, to exist at all. Heidegger noted as much in his 1915 Thesis on Duns Scotus:

Philosophy cannot do without its actual optics, metaphysics, in the long run. For the theory of truth this means the abandonment of a final metaphysical-philosophical interpretation of consciousness. In this, the value actually already lives, insofar as it is a meaningful and meaning-realizing living act, which is not remotely understood if it is neutralized into the concept of a biological blind factuality.

Kant is arguing against Secular and Protestant tendencies to commit Futurism- that is, seeing beliefs as independent and formless from it's predecessors. Jung argues the same thing- that the Hero myth which the Christian claim is rooted in originates from an elemental Psychic state, genetically universal to all humans. Hegel recognized this same fact in his Lectures on Religion: "The idea of the Incarnation, for example, runs through all religions. Such general concepts also assert themselves in other spheres of the Geist." Because it is biological, it is universal and has manifested in many forms across human history and in virtually all cultures. It is the ideological manifestation of human physiology; the dramatized representation of the emergence of human consciousness itself. The ancient archetypical death-and-resurrection Hero Archetype (the 'good dream' as St. Lewis put it)- is rooted in emergent biology and expresses itself in the deepest levels of unconscious psychology.
Specifically, the conceptualization of Christ is rooted in the Egyptian Sun-god Horus, which was a reworking of the Mesopotamian deity Marduk (who could 'speak magic words') which made it's way through the Roman iteration of Zoroastrianism, Mithraism, into Christianity. Conversely- the word 'Satan' evolved from the word Seth, the Egyptian god of Chaos. Yet the assumption that this makes the Christian claim of the Incarnation of the Theanthropos 'not true' or simply a myth like any other is itself rooted in the Nominalistic assumptions within the Western Rationalist Religion, particularly Modernism and it's current successor. Ironically, this Modernist and post-modernist argument is itself religious dogma, a dogma which was adopted from the Futuristic nature of Fundamentalist Apologists.

Jung makes the case that the emergent biological roots of the Hero-Myth make the story of Christ more than merely factually or historically true; it is super-rational, truer than true: the highest form of truth possible. Newman phrased this as "Conscience is the aboriginal Vicar of Christ, a prophet in its informations, a monarch in its peremptoriness". In other words, Consciousness contains both objective and subjective truth; the biologically ingrained Hero Myth is not an illusion of the mind, but a precept of the truest true. This primordial story only incarnated fully one time in human history across all cultures and religions. The Universal only Particularized, the Multiplicity met the Singularity, the All became the One, the unknowable became knowable and the Infinite was made manifest through Finite form only once. And nothing could be more meaningful than the Divine becoming Human because Meaning itself exists at the intersection of the Particular and the Universal. He is the discrimination of composite natures; unitemporal and eternal, unique and universal, supernatural and natural simultaneously.

Kant's apologetics follow a similar track as Jung, only along metaphysical lines instead of merely Psychological. Kant argues that the moral Atheist is incongruent to his own worship, for the very recognition of a Transcendental Good is also de facto a belief in God: "how will he [the atheist] judge his own inner purpose by the moral law which he actively worships?" For we do not hold ideas, Kant and Jung say, rather, we are held by ideas; they possess us, we do not possess them.

His aim here is to keep both natural science and theology within their respective dialectal parameters, and reconcile the antinomies of Newtonian Rationalism and Moral Teleology, as Jung says "The puddle reflecting the galaxies of the night sky" or the reconciliation of the material and the immaterial:

Two things fill my mind with new and ever-increasing admiration and awe, the more frequently and persistently my mind is occupied with them: The starry sky above me and the moral law within me. I must not look for either of them, nor merely suppose them to be veiled in darkness or exuberance, outside my range of vision; I see them before me and connect them directly with the consciousness of my existence. The first starts from the place I occupy in the outer world of the senses, and extends the connection in which I stand into the immeasurable greatness of worlds upon worlds and systems of systems, and beyond that into the boundless times of their periodic movement, their beginning and continuation.

The second starts from my invisible self, my personality, and represents me in a world that has true infinity, but is only perceptible to the mind, and with which (but also at the same time with all those visible worlds) I recognize myself, not as being there, in merely accidental, but general and necessary connection. The first sight of an innumerable number of worlds destroys, as it were, my importance, like that of an animal creature which, after having been supplied for a short time with life-force (one does not know how), has to return the matter from which it has become to the planet (a mere point in the universe).

The second, on the other hand, increases my value as an intelligence infinitely, through my personality, in which the moral law reveals to me a life independent of animality and even of the whole world of the senses, at least as much as can be deduced from the purposeful determination of my existence by this law, which is not limited to the conditions and limits of this life, but goes into infinity. ...The contemplation of the world began with the most marvelous sight that human senses can only ever present, and our intellect, in its wide scope, can only ever tolerate to pursue, and ended - with the interpretation of the stars.

Morality began with the noblest quality in human nature, the development and culture of which is aimed at infinite benefit, and ended - with enthusiasm, or superstition. So it goes with all still crude experiments, in which the noblest part of the business depends on the use of reason, which, like the use of the feet, does not find itself by means of frequent exercise, especially when it concerns qualities that cannot be so directly represented in common experience.

Timeline of Kant's Life and Works

1724 – Birth
Born on April 22 in Königsberg, Prussia (now Kaliningrad, Russia).

1730's Enlightenment
The Enlightenment, a major intellectual movement advocating reason and science, was gaining momentum across Europe.

1740 - University Enrollment
Enrolled at the University of Königsberg, initially focusing on mathematics and physics.

1748 - "An Inquiry Concerning Human Understanding" by David Hume
This significant work by Hume, emphasizing empirical skepticism, would later play a critical role in awakening Kant from his "dogmatic slumber."

1755 - Doctorate and First Book
Received his doctorate; published "General Natural History and Theory of the Heavens," proposing a nebular hypothesis of solar system formation.

1756-1764 - Academic Lectures
Began lecturing at the University of Königsberg in metaphysics and logic.

1759 - "Candide"
Perhaps Voltaire's most famous work, "Candide" is a satirical novella that criticizes the optimistic philosophies of the time, especially Leibniz's assertion that "this is the best of all possible worlds."

1763 - "Treatise on Tolerance"
Written in response to the execution of Jean Calas, this work was a powerful plea for religious tolerance and justice.

1762 – The Social Contract
Jean-Jacques Rousseau's "Emile," which profoundly influenced his philosophy, especially regarding freedom and moral law was published alongside of the Social Contract.

1770 Tenure and Latin Thesis

Kant defends his habitation defense in Latin, allowing him to become full professor and continue his work.

1781 - "Critique of Pure Reason"

Published his most famous work, which examines the relationship between human experience and knowledge, revolutionizing Western philosophy.

1783 - "Prolegomena to Any Future Metaphysics"

This work was intended to clarify the ideas presented in the "Critique of Pure Reason."

1785 - "Groundwork of the Metaphysics of Morals"

Outlined Kant's ethical philosophy, introducing the categorical imperative as the fundamental principle of morality.

1788 - "Critique of Practical Reason"

This second Critique focuses on moral philosophy and the role of free will.

1789 - French Revolution Begins

This year marks the start of the French Revolution, a significant event in European and world history, symbolizing the rise of democracy and substantial social and political changes.

1793 - Execution of Louis XVI

The French Revolution leads to the execution of King Louis XVI, symbolizing the fall of the old monarchical order and the rise of revolutionary ideals.

1790 - "Critique of Judgment"

The third Critique, dealing with aesthetics and teleology, attempting to bridge the gap between the natural world and the realm of freedom.

1793 - "Religion within the Bounds of Mere Reason"

Explored religious themes within the framework of critical philosophy, controversially arguing for a rational basis of faith.

1797 - "Metaphysics of Morals"

In this work, Kant further develops his ethical theories, divided into the "Doctrine of Right" and the "Doctrine of Virtue."

1804 - Napoleonic Code / Kant's Death

The Napoleonic Code is enacted, marking a fundamental change in the French legal system and reflecting the broader impact of the Napoleonic Wars in Europe. This year also marks the death of Immanuel Kant.

Brief Index of Kantian Terminology

Transcendental Apperception

Transcendental apperception is a complex concept in Kant's philosophy, referring to the unifying self-consciousness that underlies all our thoughts and perceptions. The self-consciousness that accompanies all concepts and all consciousness. It is the process by which the mind integrates sensory experiences into a coherent understanding of the world. This concept is central to Kant's theory of knowledge, as it explains how disparate sensory inputs are synthesized into a single, unified experience. Transcendental apperception is foundational to human cognition, enabling individuals to have a continuous and consistent experience of the self and the world. It plays a crucial role in understanding how knowledge is formed, linking sensory perceptions with the self-awareness that makes experience meaningful and coherent.

A priori / A posteriori

Distinctions between types of knowledge or justification. A priori knowledge is independent of experience (e.g., mathematical truths), while a posteriori knowledge is dependent on experience.

Analytic / Synthetic

Analytic propositions are true by virtue of their meaning, with the predicate concept contained in the subject (e.g., "All bachelors are unmarried"). Synthetic propositions are not determined by the meanings of their terms and require empirical investigation.

Categorical Imperative

A foundational concept in Kant's moral philosophy, it's a principle that one must follow regardless of desire, and it dictates that actions should be universally applicable.

Ding an sich (Thing-in-itself)

An object as it is in itself, independent of observation, which cannot be known through sensory experience.

Empirical Realism

Kant's view that although the properties of objects as we perceive them are mind-dependent, the objects themselves exist independently of our perceptions.

Transcendental Idealism
Kant's theory that human experience of things is similar to the way they appear to us, but not necessarily as they are in themselves. Our understanding is shaped by the mind's structures.

Phenomena / Noumena
Phenomena are things as they appear to us through sensory experience, whereas noumena are things as they are in themselves, which we cannot experience directly.

Hypothetical Imperative:
A command of reason that applies conditionally, depending on one's desires and goals (e.g., "If you want to be healthy, exercise regularly").

Transcendental Aesthetic:
The part of Kant's philosophy dealing with the a priori conditions of sensibility (space and time) that underlie our ability to experience phenomena.

Transcendental Deduction:
An argument in Kant's "Critique of Pure Reason" aiming to show how a priori concepts (categories) are necessary in experiencing objects.

Transcendental Unity of Apperception:
The idea that all of our representations (perceptions, thoughts, etc.) are united in a single, self-conscious experience.

Practical Reason:
The faculty of determining the will through the application of moral principles; central in Kant's ethics.

The Categorical Imperative's Formulations
Including the Formula of Universality (act only according to that maxim whereby you can at the same time will that it should become a universal law), the Formula of Humanity (act in such a way that you treat humanity, whether in your own person or in the person of another, always at the same time as an end and never simply as a means), and the Formula of the Kingdom of Ends (act according to the maxims of a universally legislating member of a merely possible kingdom of ends).

Schematism
The process by which the imagination synthesizes sensuous intuitions with a priori concepts or categories of understanding.

Transcendental Logic
A branch of logic that studies the a priori principles that make all possible empirical knowledge possible.

Moral Autonomy
Kant's idea that moral agents are self-legislating and free when they act according to moral laws they have rational reasons to endorse. It refers to the ability and responsibility of a person to make ethical decisions autonomously, or independently, based on reason and moral principles, rather than external influences or internal compulsions. This concept implies that individuals have the capability to reason and decide what is morally right or wrong, and to act accordingly. Moral autonomy is grounded in the belief that humans are inherently capable of rational thought and thus can choose to act according to universal moral laws. It rejects the idea that morality is determined by external authorities or societal norms, emphasizing instead the role of individual reasoning in ethical decision-making.

Maxim
A subjective principle of volition; the rule that the will follows when making a decision. In philosophy, a maxim is a subjective principle or rule that guides an individual's actions. It's a personal conviction or belief that a person uses to make decisions and to judge what is right or wrong. Maxims are central to the moral philosophy of Immanuel Kant, who argued that for an action to be morally good, its maxim must be universalizable. This means that one should only act according to that maxim which one can at the same time will to become a universal law. In this context, maxims are not just personal guidelines but are meant to be applicable to all rational beings. The concept of a maxim underscores the importance of intention and the principles underlying actions in moral reasoning.

Radical Evil
Radical evil, in Kantian philosophy, refers to a deep-rooted inclination in human nature that can lead individuals to prioritize

their own self-interest over moral laws. This concept challenges the optimistic view of human nature as inherently good or neutral, suggesting instead that there is a fundamental moral flaw embedded within the human condition. Kant's notion of radical evil does not imply that individuals are innately evil or incapable of moral actions. Rather, it suggests that the propensity for self-interest can lead to moral transgressions, making moral vigilance and the cultivation of virtue crucial. This concept is significant in exploring the complexities of human morality and the constant struggle between self-interest and moral duty.

Kingdom of Ends

Radical evil, in Kantian philosophy, refers to a deep-rooted inclination in human nature that can lead individuals to prioritize their own self-interest over moral laws. This concept challenges the optimistic view of human nature as inherently good or neutral, suggesting instead that there is a fundamental moral flaw embedded within the human condition. Kant's notion of radical evil does not imply that individuals are innately evil or incapable of moral actions. Rather, it suggests that the propensity for self-interest can lead to moral transgressions, making moral vigilance and the cultivation of virtue crucial. This concept is significant in exploring the complexities of human morality and the constant struggle between self-interest and moral duty.

Personalities in Kantian Philosophy

David Hume

A Scottish Enlightenment philosopher, Hume is best known for his empiricism and skepticism. His ideas, particularly on causality and the nature of knowledge, had a profound impact on Kant in an inverted manner. Hume challenged the notion of causality being an inherent property of objects and argued that our belief in causation is a result of habit rather than logical necessity. This skepticism about causality and the limitations of human understanding led Kant to critically examine the foundations of knowledge, which ultimately resulted in his famous "Copernican revolution" in philosophy.

Kant's engagement with Hume's philosophy is most evident in his work "Critique of Pure Reason," where he seeks to establish a basis for human knowledge that reconciles the rationalist and empiricist traditions. Kant famously remarked that Hume had awakened him from his "dogmatic slumber," leading him to question the very possibility of metaphysics and to reevaluate the role of reason in understanding the world.

Jean-Jacques Rousseau

Jean-Jacques Rousseau was a Genevan philosopher whose views on freedom and human nature significantly influenced Kant and the entire Enlightenment. Rousseau proposed that humans are inherently good but are corrupted by society (this idea was mocked by Voltaire openly). This idea resonated with Kant, who was grappling with the nature of morality and freedom, but ultimately disagreed with his concept of "Radical Evil". Rousseau's emphasis on the social contract and the general will also influenced Kant's ideas about autonomy and the moral law.

Rousseau's concept of freedom as adherence to a law that one has prescribed to oneself is echoed in Kant's formulation of the categorical imperative, the central principle of his moral philosophy. Kant's notion of autonomy, where an individual's actions are guided by moral law, aligns with Rousseau's idea of freedom being the adherence to a self-imposed law.

Gottfried Wilhelm Leibniz

Leibniz, a German philosopher and mathematician, was a major figure in the rationalist tradition and published incredibly important mathematical theorums, leading to Calculus. His metaphysical ideas, particularly the concept of monads and pre-established harmony, were influential in shaping Kant's early philosophical thought. Leibniz's optimism about the capacity of reason to understand the universe contrasted with Kant's later critical philosophy.

Kant disagreed with Leibniz's view that sensory experience could be reduced to rational concepts and that reality was fundamentally rational. Kant's "Critique of Pure Reason" can be seen as a response to Leibnizian rationalism, emphasizing the limits of human understanding and the role of sensory experience in shaping our knowledge.

Christian Wolff

Christian Wolff was a prominent German philosopher and a key figure in the German Enlightenment. His systematic approach to philosophy and his rationalist views were influential in Kant's early development. Wolff's method of using logical deduction to derive truths about the world provided a framework that Kant initially embraced and later critically examined.

Kant eventually moved away from Wolff's strict rationalism, developing his own critical philosophy. He criticized Wolff's approach for its failure to recognize the limits of pure reason and its overemphasis on logical deduction in understanding the world. Kant's development of transcendental philosophy, which sought to establish the conditions under which knowledge is possible, can be seen as a response to Wolff's rationalist system.

Thomas Hobbes

Thomas Hobbes, an English philosopher, was best known for his political philosophy, particularly his theory of the social contract and the nature of human self-interest. Hobbes' materialistic view of the world and his ideas about the necessity of an absolute sovereign to prevent societal collapse were influential in shaping Kant's thoughts on morality and political philosophy.

While Kant disagreed with Hobbes' pessimistic view of human nature and his advocacy for absolute monarchy, he did engage with Hobbes' ideas about the social contract. Kant's concept of the Kingdom of Ends, a society where rational beings agree upon and abide by universal moral laws, can be seen as a more optimistic reinterpretation of Hobbes' social contract theory. Kant believed in the possibility of a rational and moral social order, contrasting with Hobbes' emphasis on the need for a strong sovereign to maintain order.

John Locke

John Locke was an English philosopher whose ideas on empiricism and the theory of knowledge were a point of contrast for Kant. Locke argued that all knowledge is derived from sensory experience and that the mind at birth is a blank slate, a theory known as *tabula rasa*. This emphasis on empirical knowledge influenced Kant, who sought to reconcile rationalist and empiricist views of knowledge.

Kant diverged from Locke by arguing that while all knowledge begins with experience, not all knowledge arises from experience. In his "Critique of Pure Reason," Kant introduced the idea of a priori synthetic judgments – knowledge that is both independent of experience and provides new information. This concept was a direct response to the empirical tradition of Locke and others, asserting the role of innate structures in shaping human experience and understanding.

Baruch Spinoza

Baruch Spinoza, a Dutch philosopher, was known for his rationalistic system and monistic view of the universe, where God and nature were seen as two aspects of a single substance. Spinoza's ideas provided a counterpoint to Kant's dualistic view of the world. While Spinoza's pantheism was controversial, his rigorous logical approach to philosophy and his challenge to traditional views of morality and religion influenced Kant's philosophical development.

Kant's critical engagement with Spinoza is evident in his rejection of monism and his development of transcendental idealism, where the phenomenal world is distinguished from the noumenal world. Kant disagreed with Spinoza's dismissal of individual freedom and moral responsibility. For Kant, freedom and autonomy were central to his ethical system, contrasting with Spinoza's deterministic universe.

Isaac Newton

Newton had a significant influence on Kant's philosophy of science, as he and Leibnitz were two of the dominant scientists of that age. Newton's laws of motion and his method of empirical observation and mathematical description of nature shaped Kant's understanding of scientific knowledge and the laws of nature. Kant admired Newton's work and sought to apply a similar methodological rigor to philosophy. He believed that Newton's approach to understanding the physical world could be paralleled in understanding metaphysical principles. However, Kant also argued that while Newton's laws could describe how objects behave in space and time, they did not explain the nature of space and time themselves, leading to his own critical examination of these concepts.

René Descartes

René Descartes, a French philosopher and mathematician, was known for his method of doubt and his dualism of mind and body. Descartes' emphasis on the certainty of self-consciousness ("I think, therefore I am") and his quest for indubitable knowledge were significant in shaping Kant's epistemological inquiries. Kant critiqued Descartes' dualism and his reliance on innate ideas. Kant argued for a more complex relationship between the mind and the world, where the mind plays an active role in shaping our experience of reality. This led to Kant's distinction between phenomena (the world as we experience it) and noumena (the world as it is in itself), a pivotal element in his transcendental idealism.

Translator's Notes

Translating Immanuel Kant's philosophical works into English presents a variety of challenges, mainly due to the intrinsic complexity and specificity of his German lexicon. Kant's use of language in his original texts, particularly in seminal works such as the Critique of Pure Reason, is characterised by a dense, technical and highly nuanced use of German. His prose often employs an intricate structure of nested clauses and a lexicon that blends the technical terminology of philosophy with the evolving German language of the 18th century. This linguistic amalgamation results in passages that are notoriously difficult to render accurately in English.

The aim of this edition is to demystify Kant's complex ideas, making them more accessible to the modern reader without diluting their intellectual rigor. This translation simplifies Kant's complex language, making it as accessible as possible. Footnotes are removed, and difficult terminology is translated as literally as possible. Complex sentences are also simplified, while ensuring the philosophical integrity of Kant's ideas remains intact. This method aims to make Kant's deep ideas more readable to a broader audience without compromising their original depth, bridging the gap between scholarly study and general interest in Kant's philosophy.

Difficult German words are translated into English in the most literal way possible, even if they seem strange to English speakers. Words like "Mien" (continuance or appearance) and "Phlegmatisch" (stoic disposition) are used intentionally by Kant to convey specific concepts. Similarly, terms like 'assertoric' and 'apodeictic' from Aristotelian logic are preserved to maintain the philosophical rigor and authenticity of Kant's work. This approach allows readers to engage with the complexity of Kant's thought in its original form, respecting the intellectual challenge of his work.

Kant's writing style, characterized by long, complex sentences with multiple embedded clauses, poses significant challenges. This syntactic complexity is a feature of German grammar that allows complex ideas to be expressed in a single sentence. However, such sentence structures are less natural in English, leading translators to either simplify the syntax, which risks diluting the complexity and depth of Kant's arguments, or retain the original structure, which can result in unwieldy and difficult-to-read English prose. This dichotomy forces translators to constantly balance fidelity to the original text against the need for clarity and readability in the target language.

The historical and philosophical context of Kant's work adds another layer of difficulty. Kant wrote in a specific intellectual milieu, influenced by the blossoming Enlightenment and responding to the works of predecessors such as David Hume and contemporaries such as Johann Gottlieb Fichte. His language reflects these influences and dialogues, requiring translators to be not only skilled linguists but also well versed in the philosophical discourse of the time. This context-specific language often lacks direct equivalents in modern English, requiring interpretation to convey the underlying philosophical discourse and historical nuances.

As such, this translation also retains certain Latin and French references to reflect Kant's original intent. Latin terms like 'schema' and 'atoma' refer to concepts in Cartesian and Newtonian philosophy. These references connect modern readers to the historical and philosophical contexts of Kant's time, and remain untranslated to keep this connection to the original concepts they represent, as Kant intended.

"In a famous saying the philosopher Kant calls the existence of the starry sky and that of the moral law in our breast as the strongest witnesses for the greatness of God. As strange as this composition sounds - for what may the heavenly bodies have to do with the question whether a human child loves or kills another? - it nevertheless touches on a great psychological truth."

Sigmund Freud

NEWCOMB LIVRARIA
- P R E S S -

Made in the USA
Monee, IL
04 July 2024

61192445R00050